CINZIA VALIGI

ROME
and
VATICAN

Published and printed by

plurigraf

NARNI - TERNI

Introduction

«All roads lead to Rome»: so goes an old saying in praise of the grandeur and importance of a city which claimed for itself the title of «caput mundi». And, by the same token, whatever road the visitor has taken to reach it, he can be sure that what he is about to be offered is an opportunity to admire and study an historical, artistic and monumental heritage of universal value. For Roman civilization was, together with that of Greece, the great cradle of Western Civilization. If the Greeks gave the best of themselves in literature, art, philosophy and the life of the spirit, the Romans, with their greater practical and rational sense, devoted themselves rather to political life, administration and the organization of the Empire. This difference in character is reflected in their works: while those of the Greeks pursue an ideal of pure harmony and beauty, those of the Romans are imbued with a sense of grandeur, power and a more frankly utilitarian spirit. This, indeed, is the main characteristic of Roman architecture, whose fascination will inevitably be exerted on visitors during their visits to the Roman Forums, the Amphitheatres, the Basilicas and the triumphal arches.

By a strange and uniquely privileged destiny, History conspired to ensure that, even after the fall of the Roman Empire, in less glorious times than those of the Caesars, Rome should preserve its role as a source of civilization and as a cultural and moral centre of the world by becoming the capital of Christianity and the Apostolic See of the Successor of Peter. It was precisely due to the Papacy that the city revived during the Renaissance period and expressed a cultural and artistic activity which it had not had since the days of antiquity. The new splendour of Rome found its greatest expression in the building of the new Basilica of St. Peter and the vast complex of the Vatican Palaces with their incomparable masterpieces of Bramante, Raphael and Michelangelo which represent some of the greatest artistic achievements of all time.

The city of Rome is thus the witness *par excellence* to the millennial history of the West, and a thorough description of its notable monumental heritage would require a work that would fill a library in itself. The guide we here present to you has thus been conceived according to criteria of conciseness and simplicity. Its aim is to provide the reader with all that is essential to enable him or her to tune into the living breath of History, the eternal fascination, that the city emanates from its every ruin, its every work of art.

The Piazza Venezia

Situated at the centre of Rome, the piazza is one of the most scenic in the whole city. Rectangular in shape, its focal point is the **Victor Emanuel Monument**: the huge marble « wedding-cake » raised to the first king of united Italy, Vittorio Emanuele II. The piazza is the point of confluence of the city's most important streets: the Via del Corso, the Via Quattro Novembre, the Via del Plebiscito which leads by way of the Corso Vittorio Emanuele to St. Peter's, and the Via dei Fori Imperiali, which flanks the ancient ruins of the Roman Forum and leads to the Colosseum. The piazza, thanks to its central position, is a convenient point of departure for various tourist itineraries.

The Palazzo Venezia

The Victor Emanuel II monument

The Palazzo Venezia

Built for Cardinal Pietro Barbo, later to become Pope Paul II, in 1455, the palace is attributed by some scholars to the distinguished Renaissance architect **Leon Battista Alberti**. Considered one of the very first buildings in the Renaissance style in the city, it is very austere in appearance and presents a brown-stuccoed façade relieved by three orders of windows in white marble; particularly striking are those in the shape of a Guelf cross on the first floor. The building now houses the interesting **Museum** of the Palazzo Venezia which contains important medieval and Renaissance works of art, and collections of porcelain and silver dating to various periods.

Particularly noteworthy is the Throne Room (Sala Regia) in which are displayed precious Flemish, German and Italian tapestries of the 15th and 16th century and a magnificent series of arms and armour datable from the 9th to the 16th century. The silverware collection is displayed in two rooms and comprises some fine examples of gold and silversmith's work, including such genuine masterpieces as the **Orsini Cross** (1334) and the **Triptych of Alba Fucense.**

The Basilica of S. Marco

Annexed to the Palazzo Venezia is the **Basilica of San Marco**, founded in the 4th century, but completely reconstructed, after various interventions, by Cardinal Pietro Barbo in 1455-71. The façade, in elegant Renaissance style, probably designed by **Giovanni Da Maiano**, is adorned by a handsome portico formed of three arcades surmounted by the Loggia of the Benediction.

The interior, after its restoration by F. Barigioni between 1740 and 1750, is decorated in a pure baroque style. But of the Renaissance church the beautiful wooden coffered ceiling, the work of Giovannino and Marco de' Dolci, survives.

Some wonderful 9th mosaics depicting Christ, the Apostles and some saints are preserved in the apse. Displayed in the Sacristy are a 15th century altar by Mino da Fiesole and a painting of the Evangelist St. Mark by Melozzo da Forlì. Outside the basilica, in the Piazzetta San Marco, stands one of the so-called « speaking statues of the city » — the mouthpiece of satirical pasquinades — popularly known as **Madama Lucrezia**: the statue is thought to represent the goddess Isis.

The Victor Emanuel Monument

The colossal white monument dedicated to the memory of Italy's first king, Vittorio Emanuele II, and also known as the **Vittoriano**, stands out clearly in the background of the Piazza Venezia. Designed by Giuseppe Sacconi and erected to commemorate the unification of Italy after the Risorgimento, it celebrates the great patriotic and military values which had triumphed to forge Italy into a single Nation. The monument was begun in 1885, but was not completed till forty years later. The vast central stairway leads to the **Altar of the Nation** with the Tomb of the Unknown Soldier which contains the remains of an unnamed soldier who died fighting for the country during the First World War; two sentinels keep constant guard over it. Above the shrine, placed within a niche, is the statue of Roma, flanked on either side by celebratory reliefs: to the left the Triumphal Processions of Work, and to the right Patriotic Love, sculpted by Angelo Zanelli.

To the side of the ceremonial staircase are two fountains representing the Tyrrhenian Sea (to the right) and the Adriatic Sea (to the left).

In front of the latter are the remains of the Tomb of Publicius Bibulus, dating to the 1st century B.C.

At the centre of the monument stands the colossal equestrian

statue of Victor Emanuel, the work of **Enrico Chiaradia**. The statue is supported on a large plinth decorated with symbolic sculptures of the most important cities of Italy, the work of **Maccagnini**. Above, a wide arcaded colonnade is decorated with a series of figures representing the regions of Italy, and completed by two lateral propylaea bearing huge bronze chariots with Winged Victories at their reins. Inside, the Monument houses the Institute for the History of the Italian Risorgimento, the Library and the Central Museum of the Risorgimento with archive annexed.

The Piazza del Campidoglio - Marcus Aurelius

The Capitoline

In ancient times the focal point of religious life, the Capitoline, the most famous of the seven hills of Rome, constitutes the area where the most significant events in the history of the city took place.

The hill consists of two summits, at the centre of which now extends the Piazza del Campidoglio, at one time the **asylum**, i.e. the area granted by Romulus to the plebs. On one of the two heights now stands the church of Santa Maria in Aracoeli, its site occupied in ancient times by the Capitoline Shrine. On the other stood the great Temple of Jupiter Optimus Maximus. From the steep cliffs of the southern part of the hill, known in ancient times as **Mons Tarpeius** — the Tarpeian Rock —, traitors of the country were thrown to their death; remains of the Temple of Jupiter can be seen close to it.

The architectural complex of the Piazza del Campidoglio, now the centre of the public life of the city, owes its harmonious appearance to the genius of **Michelangelo**, who designed it for Pope Paul III.

The Piazza del Campidoglio

Conceived by the great mind of the artist, the piazza consists of a trapezoidal space delimited by three palaces: on the right the Palazzo dei Conservatori; on the left the Palazzo Nuovo (or Capitoline Museum); and on the side to the rear the Palazzo Senatorio (Senator's Palace). The piazza is approached by an imposing staircase (the Cordonata), it too bearing the impress of **Michelangelo**. At its foot are two lions of Egyptian porphyry. At the head of the stairs are the colossal statues of the **Dioscuri**, Castor and Pollux with their horses; they are flanked, along the balustrade, by the **Trophies of Marius**, the statues of Constantine and Constantine II, and, at the end, two milestone columns brought from the Via Appia. Particularly famous is the equestrian **statue of Marcus Aurelius** set up on a plinth at the centre of the Piazza. According to some sources, the statue, cast in bronze in the 2nd century A.D., was brought here from the Lateran by Pope Paul III in 1538, contrary to Michelangelo's plan. According to tradition, the statue has survived only because it was thought to represent the emperor Constantine.

Plastic model of the ancient Rome - The Campidoglio

The Piazza del Campidoglio (Michelangelo)

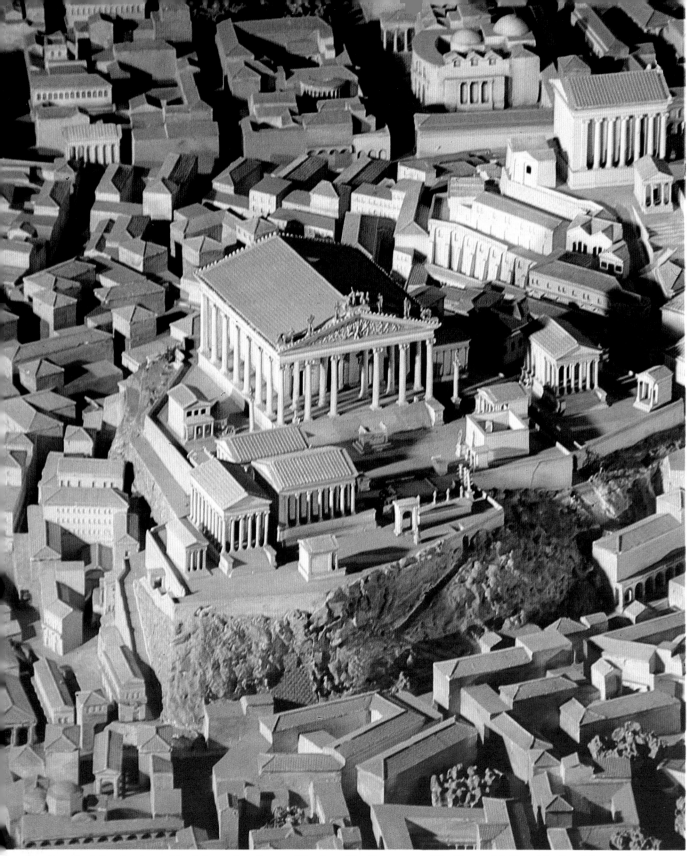

Detail of the plastic model of the ancient Rome - The Campidoglio

The Piazza del Campidoglio - Marcus Aurelius ➤

The Palazzo Senatorio

The palace, now the Town Hall and seat of the municipal council of Rome, faces onto the piazza with an imposing façade. At its base is a double stairway, below which — at the centre of its twin ramps — is a niche containing a **statue of the Goddess Roma** who holds an orb in her hand, emblem of the rule of Rome over the world. She is flanked by two colossal statues of river-gods representing the Nile and the Tigris, the latter later transformed into the Tiber. The palace was built on the site of the ancient **Tabularium**. Behind it rises the bell-tower, erected by Martino Longhi the Elder in the 16th century. A series of large and interesting rooms are contained inside the Palazzo Senatorio; among the most famous are the **Room of the Banners**, the **Council Hall** dominated by its statue of Julius Caesar, and the **Protomoteca Capitolina**, a collection of busts of famous men installed here in 1950.

By descending the Via del Campidoglio to the side of the Palazzo Senatorio, we can see the remains of the famous Temple of Vejove, an ancient Italic deity, which came to light during the work of reconstruction.

Mosaic of the Doves

The Palazzo Nuovo

The building, situated to the left of the Piazza del Campidoglio, was designed by **Michelangelo** on the model of the Palazzo dei Conservatori facing it on the other side of the piazza. It was only built in the 17th century, when it was decided to enhance the piazza's perspective effect and so give it the harmoniousness and coherence that distinguish it today. The Palazzo Nuovo now houses the **Capitoline Museum**, which contains an ancient collection of works of sculpture of the classical period. In the courtyard is the **Fountain of Marforio** formed of the colossal recumbent statue of a river-god, another of the so-called «speaking statues» of the city which, in the placards appended of them, pilloried the follies of the age. The collection of ancient statuary originally housed in the Palazzo dei Conservatori on the opposite side of the piazza was removed here in the mid-17th century. In the Atrium of the ground-floor is the important **statue of Minerva** (5th century B.C.). To the left of the courtyard is the **Egyptian Collection**, while the Atrium is flanked by two suites of rooms: the **Groundfloor Rooms to the right,** with the Amendola sarcophagus (2nd century); and the **Groundfloor Rooms to the left,** which comprise interesting statues relating to oriental cults.

Ascending to the first floor, consisting of seven rooms, we first enter a wide **Gallery** which runs the whole length of the building and in which a series of interesting statues are displayed, including the beautiful statue of the goddess **Athena** found in Velletri near Rome; a fine **head of the emperor Probus**; and a statue of **Amor drawing a bow.**

Room of the Doves: it derives its name from a mosaic attributed to Sosus of Pergamon representing four doves drinking from a vase. The room also contains the sarcophagus of a child and the **Tabula Iliaca**, a relief of the destruction of Troy.

Cabinet of Venus: it contains the Capitoline Venus, a wonderful statue of the goddess dating to the 2nd century B.C., but a copy of an earlier statue.

Room of the Emperors: it contains 65 busts of Roman em-

Capitoline Venus

Hall Orazi and Curiazi

The Dying Gaul

perors, constituting one of the richest and finest collections of its kind, also from the point of view of the iconography of the imperial period.

Room of the Philosophers: it takes its name from a series of portrait busts of Greek and Roman thinkers and philosophers, such as those representing Socrates, Cicero, Homer and the orator Lysias.

Saloon: this, the largest room on the first floor, contains a copy of the Centaurs, dating to the Hadrianic period, and the beautiful statue of a wounded Amazon, a copy of the original by Kresilas.

Room of the Faun: it contains Roman inscriptions (including the **lex de imperio Vespasiani**: the bronze tablet conferring imperial power on Vespasian), and the statue of a laughing Faun holding a bunch of grapes to his mouth.

Room of the Dying Gaul: at the centre of the room is the statue of a dying Gaulish warrior, found in the Orti Sallustiani.

The Palazzo dei Conservatori

The palace, rebuilt by **Giacomo Della Porta** in the 16th century based on **Michelangelo's** design, contains the **Halls of the Conservators,** the **Museum of the Palazzo dei Conservatori,** the **Braccio Nuovo** (or new wing), the **Museo Nuovo** and the **Capitoline Picture Gallery.**

The courtyard contains the colossal head of the emperor Constantine, recovered from the Basilica of Constantine, as well as some interesting reliefs.

We now ascend to the first floor and enter the first of the Halls of the Conservators:

Hall of the Horatii and Curatii: it takes its name from a fresco depicting one of the battles between **Horatii and Curatii**. The room also contains statues of Urban VIII (Bernini) and Innocent X (Algardi).

Through the **Room of the Captains**, we enter the **Room of the Triumphs**: at its centre is the famous bronze statue of a boy pulling a thorn out of his foot, known as the **Spinario**, dating to the ist century B.C.

Room of the Wolf: it houses the famous **Capitoline Wolf**, a bronze statue dating to the 5th century B.C. which has, since time immemorial, been the symbol of Rome. The figures of Romulus and Remus being suckled by the Wolf were added by Antonio Pollaiuolo in the 15th century.

A series of other rooms follow, richly decorated with sculptures, friezes and valuable 18th century tapestries.

The Museum of the Palazzo dei Conservatori

Especially noteworthy among its important holdings of classical statues, inscriptions, valuable collections of Greek and Etruscan vases and numerous sarcophagi are: the marble statue known as the **Esquiline Venus** (Gallery of the Orti Lamiani), an elaborately decorated bronze funerary bed (Room of the Bronzes), and a statue of Artemis (Room of the Magistrates).

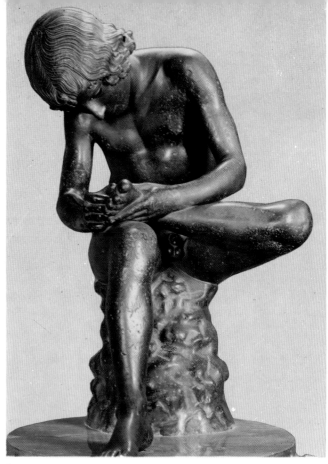

Shepherd Matius

Persian Sibyl

Hall she-wolf

Capitoline she-wolf

The Braccio Nuovo

The Braccio Nuovo, or New Wing, was installed in 1950-52 to house additional antique statuary, especially the archaeological remains found during the excavations of the Temple of Jupiter Capitolinus: they include some of its foundations and various sculptures, including the beautiful statue of Apollo as an archer, a Greek original of the 5th century B.C. (Room IV). Also worth noting, in Room I, is an ancient example of Roman painting dating to the 3rd century B.C.

The Museo Nuovo

The Museo Nuovo (New Museum) was installed in the Palazzo dei Conservatori in 1925 to house interesting Roman and Greek remains of various periods found during the repeated archaeological excavations conducted in the city from 1870 on. The Museum, which consists of ten rooms, contains magnificent examples of Greek art, such as the impressive headless statue of **Aphrodite**, probably a work of Praxiteles, and the bust of Domitian, a Roman work.

The Capitoline Picture Gallery

One thing we should on no account miss during our visit to the Capitol is the Capitoline Picture Gallery (**Pinacoteca Capitolina**), which contains important paintings from the Sacchetti and Pio collections.
Founded by Pope Benedict XIV in 1784, it includes famous paintings by **Rubens** («Romulus and Remus suckled by the Wolf»), **Diego Velazquez** («Portrait of an Unknown Man»), and **Caravaggio** («St. John the Baptist»), as well as works by many other artists of the 16th, 17th and 18th century.
A distinguished collection of 18th century porcelain is on display in the Cini Gallery.

St. John the Baptist (Caravaggio)

Romulus and Remus Suckled by the she-wolf (P.P. Rubens)

The Church of Santa Maria in Aracoeli

Occupying the summit of the Capitoline Arx (or Acropolis), it is approached by a long votive stairway built by the population in 1348 to thank the Virgin Mary for averting the threat of the plague.

According to tradition, the church stands on the site where Augustus saw the apparition of a woman with a child who said, pointing to the altar where she was sitting: «Ecce ara primogeniti Dei».: a prophecy of the coming of Our Lord. Officiated by the Franciscan Friars Minor since 1250, the church boasts of very ancient origins; in fact it was erected over the ruins of the Temple of Juno Moneta. In the 10th century it assumed the name of Santa Maria in Capitolio, which it retained till the 13th century.

The unadorned brick façade has three portals, of which the two lateral ones are adorned with lunettes bearing 16th century reliefs. The interior, consisting of a nave and two aisles divided by 22 antique marble columns, is notable for its fine medieval cosmatesque pavement and sumptuous 16th century coffered ceiling, celebrating the victory over the Turks at the naval battle of Lepanto.

The many funerary monuments contained in the church include the monument to Cardinal Ludovico d'Albret sculpted by Andrea Bregno in 1465, and a tomb slab sculpted by Donatello. The first chapel to the right, dedicated to St. Bernardine, is decorated with wonderful frescoes by **Pinturicchio** depicting the saint. Between the nave and the transepts are two fine pulpits sculpted by Lorenzo and Giacomo Cosma in the 13th century. In the right transept is the tomb of Luca Savelli (reusing a Roman sarcophagus). The baroque high altar is adorned with a beautiful painting of the Virgin Mary. In the left transept is the monument to Cardinal Matteo d'Acquasparta, probably a work of Giovanni di Cosma. In the Sacristy is housed the venerated wooden statue of the Infant Jesus known as the **Bambino dell'Aracoeli**, before which, during the Christmas period, prayers and religious songs are recited by children from far and wide.

The church of Santa Maria in Aracoeli

The Roman Forum

In ancient times the Forum was a civic piazza surrounded by basilicas, temples and monuments where the public life of the city took place. The area on which it arose was originally insalubrious and prone to flooding, but was reclaimed by various attempts at drainage over the years. The first of these was made by king Tarquinius Priscus with the construction of the **Cloaca Massima**. The place became, thanks to its position, a favourite meeting-point between the inhabitants of the city and those from the surrounding hills who saw in it an ideal market-place for selling their wares. Around this trading activity, a series of shops, temples and basilicas progressively arose, eventually transforming the area into the heart of the city, the focal point round which not only the business transactions but more especially the public life of the Roman citizen revolved. It was here that the assemblies of the people and the Senate, the elections of magistrates, the great religious ceremonies and the administration of justice took place. The enormous economic and political expansion of the city meant that the Roman Forum itself became inadequate to cope with its needs and determined the construction of others (the Imperial Forums: see below).

In 283 A.D. what had progressively grown into a monumental complex was devastated by fire; the restoration set in hand by Diocletian did not, however, mark the end of its decline or arrest its decay which continued irresistibly through the Middle Ages, hastened both by the barbarian invasions and the continuous spoliation of its materials for use in the construction of private houses and fortified strongholds. Eventually it was reduced to a pasture for cattle. Only in the 18th century did interest revive in this wonderful complex, testified by excavations and the archaeological exploration that is still continuing to this day.

The Roman Forum can be entered from the Via dei Fori Imperiali, which starts out from the Piazza Venezia to the left of the Victor Emanuel Monument. Or we can approach it by descending from the Capitoline Hill down the Clivus Capitolinus and then taking the Via del Foro Romano.

This second itinerary enables us to visit the complex consisting of the Porticus of the Dii Consentes, the Temple of Vespasian, the Temple of Concord and the Mamertine Prison.

The first monument we notice, to the left of the Clivus Capitolinus, immediately below the Tabularium, is the **Porticus of the Dii Consentes**, where 12 statues representing the main deities of Rome were placed. Only the remains of some columns survive of the Porticus.

Close to it is the **Temple of Vespasian** erected by Domitian in 81 A.D. It is testified by the presence of three wonderful marble columns in the Corinthian style.

Adjacent to it, on the Via del Foro Romano, is the **Temple of Concord**, so called because it celebrated the end of hostilities between patricians and plebeians. Built in 367 B.C., it was reconstructed by Tiberius; but only a few ruins of it remain today.

Close to it stands the **church of San Giuseppe dei Falegnami**, the church of the guild of carpenters built in 1598. Below it is the famous **Mamertine Prison**, which consists of two superimposed dungeons: the Carcer Mamertinus (2nd century B.C.)

Mamertine Prison ➤

**Roman Forum
- The Curia, The Arch
of Septimius Severus
and the Temple of
Saturn**

**Reconstruction of the
Forum**

**Plastic model of the ➤
ancient Rome - Detail**

**Roman Forum
- The Curia, The Arch
of Septimius Severus
and the Temple of
Saturn**

**Reconstruction of the
Forum**

**Plastic model of the ➤
ancient Rome - Detail**

CONSTANTINUS – 312-337 d.C.

CONSTANTINUS – (Versus)

HADRIANUS – 117 - 138 d.C.

C.I. CAESAR – 100 a.C. - 44 a.C.

1 Cestius Bridge
2 Tiber Island
3 Fabricius' Bridge
4 Emilianus' Bridge
5 Cattle Market
6 Temple of Hercules the Victor
7 Janus
8 Marcellus' Theatre
9 Vegetable Market
10 Capitolin Temple of Jupiter
11 Julius' Basilica
12 Septimius Severus' Arch
13 Curia
14 Emilianus Basilica
15 Antoninius' Temple
16 Temple of the divine Romulus
17 Temple of Peace
18 Maxentius' Basilica
19 Temple of Venus
20 Temple of Heliogabalus
21 Temple of Cybele
22 Temple of Apollo on the Palatine
23 Domus Hadriana
24 Domus Augustana
25 Hippodrome of Domitian
26 Septimius Severus Baths
27 Palace of Septimius Severus
28 Septizodium
29 Circus Maximus
30 Aqueduct of Claudius
31 Constantine's Arch
32 Nero's Colossus
33 Colosseum
34 Titus' Baths
35 Trajan's Baths
36 Temple of the divine Claudius

A plastic model of the ancient Rome by I. Gismondi - Kept in the Museum of the Roman Civilization

and the Carcer Tullianum (3rd century B.C.). It was a place of imprisonment and death for many historical personages, such as the Gaulish king Vercingetorix and the king of Numidia Jugurtha the one put to death by Julius Caesar, the other starved to death by Marius. According to the legend, another prisoner incarcerated here was St. Peter, who worked a miracle by making a fountain of water spring from the floor, so that he might have water to baptize his gaolers after having converted them to Christianity. It is from this legend that the name San Pietro in Carcere, by which the building is also called, derives.

Facing it, on the other side of the road, is the **church of Santi Luca e Martina**, consisting of two superimposed churches; the lower one was founded in honour of St. Martin in the 6th century; the upper one dates to the 17th century. The handsome travertine façade is by Pietro da Cortona.

We now approach the main entrance to the Roman Forum, which is located on the Via dei Fori Imperiali. To the right of the **Via Sacra**, the road which connected the various parts of the Forum and of which the original Roman paving is still visible, we see the remains of the **Basilica Aemilia**. The first basilica on the site was founded by M. Fulvius Nobilior and M. Aemilius Lepidus in 179 B.C., and was later reconstructed and enriched by other members of the gens Aemilia. The term basilica in ancient Rome denoted a large rectangular building in whose interior two or four rows of columns delimited a central nave and side aisles (a similar kind of plan was later adopted for the construction of Christian basilicas). Originally secular in purpose, it was assigned to business transactions and the administration of justice.

Adjacent to the Basilica Aemilia is the **Curia** or Senate House. Originally built as an assembly hall by Tullus Hostilius, it was reconstructed under Diocletian, and later, in the 7th century, converted into a church. Inside, the marble floor has been restored, and the marble podia on which the wooden benches of the Senators were placed are visible.

Almost in front of the Curia we may see the **Plutei of Trajan**, the marble parapets or screens which decorated the tribune of the Rostra. They are sculpted with scenes celebrating some important enterprises of Trajan's government — such as the provision made by the Emperor for the children of poor citizens — and reliefs of the principal sacrificial animals. The square in front of the Curia was in fact the **Comitium**: the place where the people gathered in assemblies to elect the magistrates and to decide on the major questions of political life.

On the edge of the Comitium, in front of the Curia, below a large paved area in black marble (**Lapis Niger**), is an underground shaft believed to be the **Tomb of Romulus**; an inscription of the 6th century B.C., the oldest so far found in the city, was preserved in it.

The magnificent triumphal arch just beyond it is the **Arch of Septimius Severus**. It was dedicated by the People and the Senate to the emperor Septimius Severus and his sons Caracalla and Geta in 203 to celebrate their victories over the Parthians, the Arabs and the Assyrians. Consisting of a central arch and two side arches, it is well-preserved and decorated with reliefs representing episodes from the wars conducted by Severus. Close to it is the **Umbilicus Urbis**, a circular base which indicated the centre of the city.

◄ **Plastic model of the ancient Rome - Detail**

Roman Forum

1 - The Temple of Saturne
2 - Via Sacra
3 - The Temple of Vespasianus
4 - The Rostrums

5 - The Arch of Septimius Severus
6 - The Curia
7 - Basilica Emilia
8 - Basilica of Maxentius

9 - The Temple of Antonius and Faustina
10 - The Colosseum
11 - The Round Temple of Romulus
12 - The Column of Foca

13 - **The Temple of Julius Caesar**
14 - **The Temple of Venus and Rome**
15 - **The Arch of Titus**
16 - **Temple of Vesta**

17 - **The House of the Vestal Virgins**
18 - **The Temple of Castor and Pollux**
19 - **The Church of Santa Maria Antigua**
20 - **The Palatine Hill**

21 - **The Temple of Augustus**
22 - **Basilica Giulia**

FORO ROMANO - RICOSTRUZIONE

Romanum Forum - Reconstruction

1 - The Curia	5 - The Temple of Antonius and	8 - The Temple of Venus and Rome
2 - The Arc of Septimius Severus	Faustina	9 - The Temple of Julius Caesar
3 - Basilica Emilia	6 - The Colosseum	10 - The Arc of Titus
4 - Basilica of Maxentius	7 - The Round Temple of Romulus	11 - The House of the Vestal Virgins

12 - The Church of
     Santa Maria Antigua
13 - The Palatine Hill
14 - The Temple of Augustus

15 - The Temple of Vesta
16 - The Temple of Castor and Pollux
17 - Basilica Giulia
18 - The Column of Foca

19 - The Rostrums
20 - Via Sacra
21 - The Temple of Saturne

To the left of the arch we may note a tufa wall: it is all that remains of the original platform that served as the orators' tribune. The structure is called the **Rostra** because it was adorned with the bronze beaks (*rostra*) stripped from enemy ships conquered in battle.

In front of it is a small piazza (Piazza del Foro) in which stands the **Column of Phocas** (608), the last to be erected in honour of an eastern Emperor.

To the right of the Piazza del Foro we can see the remains of the **Basilica Julia**, built by Julius Caesar. Adjacent to it are the imposing remains of the **Temple of Saturn**, built in c. 500 B.C., and reconstructed in 42 B.C. The statue of the god Saturn — ancient god of the Capitol — was venerated inside it. It also served as the State Treasury. The eight columns with Ionic capitals that remain are those of the pronaos.

By taking the Via Sacra right to the end of the Piazza del Foro we come to the few remains of the **Temple of Julius Caesar**, erected on the site where the body of Caesar was cremated and where Mark Anthony read out his famous testament.

Close to it is the basement of the **Arch of Augustus**, and to its right we can see three wonderful fluted columns of the Corinthian order which formed part of the **Temple of Castor and Pollux**. It was built in honour of the Dioscuri who, according to the legend, helped the Romans in their victory over the Latins and the Tarquins at the battle of Lake Regillus.

In its immediate vicinity is the **Lacus Juturnae** where Castor and Pollux watered their horses when they brought the news of the victory to the Romans.

Behind is the **Oratory of the Forty Martyrs** and, to its left, **Santa Maria Antiqua**, the oldest Christian building of the Forum. It was built over a building of the imperial period, reconstructed and dedicated to Christian worship in the 6th century. Of considerable artistic interest are the frescoes that adorn its walls.

Returning to the Arch of Augustus, we can see the remains of the **Regia**: seat of the Pontifex Maximus and of the archive of the annals compiled of the salient events in Roman public life. According to tradition, it occupies the site of the house of Numa Pompilius, second king of Rome.

In front of the Regia stood the **Temple of Vesta**, which can be recognised by its circular basement. It was in this temple that the sacred fire, symbolizing the life of Rome, was preserved. Guarded by the Vestals, priestesses of the goddess Vesta, the fire was constantly kept alight, for it was considered a bad omen for the destiny of the city if it should ever go out. Adjacent to the circular temple was the **House of the Vestals**, the sanctuary in which the young priestesses, guardians of the sacred fire, dwelt.

Facing the Regia on the other side of the Via Sacra is the **Temple of Antoninus and Faustina**, erected in 141 A.D. in honour of the wife of Antoninus Pius and, on the latter's death, of the emperor himself: husband and wife are commemorated in the surviving inscription on the architrave. In the 11th century the temple was converted into the **church of San Lorenzo in Miranda**.

To the right of the temple is the site of an **archaic cemetery**, with burials dating to the Early Iron Age.

This is followed, on the Via Sacra, by the **Temple of Romulus**, circular in plan and dedicated to the deified son of Maxentius.

At the end of the Via Sacra is the **Arch of Titus**, consisting of a single archway. It was erected by Domitian to commemorate the victories of Vespasian and his son Titus over the Jews and the destruction of Jerusalem.

Basilica of Maxentius

Basilica of Maxentius (Reconstruction)

➤ **Temple and house of the Vestals**

➤ **Temple and house of the Vestals (Reconstruction)**

The Arch of Titus

The Arch of Titus - Detail

The Palatine

The Palatine is the hill on which the original nucleus of the city of Rome arose: the settlement (known as « Roma quadrata ») founded by Romulus, according to legend, in 754 or 753 B.C.

The hill originally had two summits: the Palatium and the Germalus (subsequently levelled by Domitian). Of the seven hills of Rome it is undoubtedly the richest and most evocative in historical remains.

In the Republican period, many famous personalities of the time, including Cicero, built their houses on this hill. It became the site of numerous temples and, in the imperial period, also of the palaces of the emperors. The first of these latter was that of Tiberius: the domus Tiberiana.

After the decline and fall of the Roman Empire, the architectural history of the Palatine continued in the 11th century, with the building of churches, castles and convents over the ruins of antiquity, and then in the 16th when the Farnese built the sumptuous Villa Farnese and its elaborate gardens, the Orti Farnesiani, on the hill. This noble family also deserves merit for bringing the Palatine's ancient ruins to light, even though the proper archaeological exploration of the hill had to await the more systematic excavations of Rosa, Vaglieri and Boni in the 19th century.

We ascend the Palatine from the Roman Forum, by way of the Clivus Capitolinus, which we join just after the Arch of Titus. We then come to the imposing 16th century **Portal** designed by Vignola, which precedes the wonderful gardens of the **Orti Farnesiani** in which the **Farnese Pavilion**, part of their splendid villa, stands.

This delightful setting is made particularly evocative by the presence of the ancient ruins we pass during our exploration of the hill.

Of the **Domus Tiberiana**, the palace of the emperor Tiberius, little remains to be seen above ground, though it was supported by a huge artificial terrace.

Of the **Temple of Magna Mater** or **of Cybele**, whose statue now stands in the Domus Tiberiana, the podium remains. Close to it are the remains of the **Scalae Caci**, a stairway giving access to the Palatine and of very ancient origin, and some remains of prehistoric huts: according to legend, they mark the site of the **House of Romulus**. Also extant are two circular cisterns dating to the 5th century B.C., and some remains which are attributed by tradition to Rome's first circuit of walls. From the Temple of Magna Mater we make our way down to the **House of Livia**: it was in fact the house of Augustus (Livia was his wife). Its structure and the marvellous mural paintings that decorated its rooms have been preserved almost intact. Close to it is an underground passageway that connected the imperial palaces: the **Cryptoporticus of Nero**.

Beyond it are the impressive ruins of the **Domus Flavia**, the large and elaborate palace built by the Flavian emperors, notably Domitian. Various parts of the complex are well-preserved: the basilica, the Aula Regia or throne-room and the emperor's dining-room: the imperial **Triclinium**.

A convent was built over the ruins of another adjacent palace, the **Domus Augustana**: it now houses the Antiquarium of the Palatine, a museum comprising a collection of artefacts, sculptures and remains of mural paintings found on the hill.

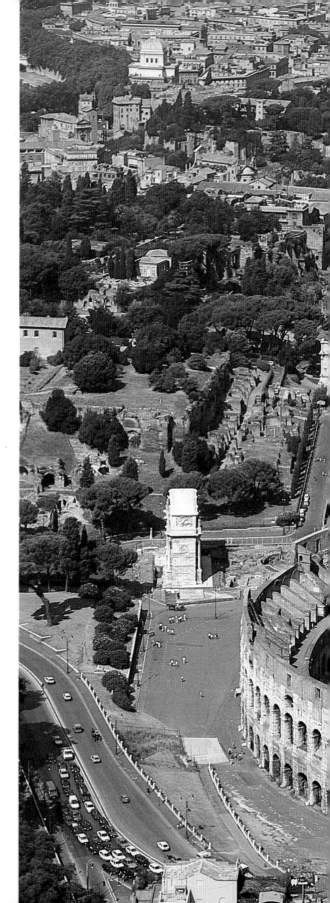

Plastic model of the ancient Rome - The Circus Maximus

Other ruins on the Palatine include the large **Hippodrome** or Stadium built by Domitian; the large and impressive remains of the **Domus Severiana**, part of the palace built by Septimius Severus; and the **Paedagogium**, a college for imperial pages also dating to the period of Domitian.

The Circus Maximus   **The Circus Maximus (Reconstruction)**

The Imperial Forums

The enormous political and economic expansion of Rome, and the consequent growth in judicial activity, meant that a single Forum was inadequate to cope with the increasing demands placed upon it (the Roman Forum, in any case, could not be enlarged due to the lack of building space).

It was Caesar who first built another one, towards the end of the Republic: this was the Forum Julium, laid out in the environs of the Campus Martius. This was followed by the successive addition of the Forum of Augustus, the Forum of Vespasian, the Forum of Nerva and the Forum of Trajan.

Our visit to the Imperial Forums has the Piazza Venezia as its departure point. Turning into the Via dei Fori Imperiali to the left of the Victor Emanuel Monument, we immediately come to the Piazza del Foro Traiano, on which two adjacent churches stand: the Renaissance **church of Santa Maria di Loreto** and the 18th century **church of the Holy Name of Mary**. Facing them are the wonderful remains of the **Forum of Trajan**, designed by Apollodorus of Damascus and built between 107 and 113: it was thus the last of the Imperial Forums to be built. Grandiose in conception, it was laid out round a central square, which was flanked by two lateral arcades; the complex of the **Basilica Ulpia** and the **Libraries**; and, on the opposite side, the **Temple of Trajan**. At the centre of the square stood an equestrian statue of the emperor. To one side of the Basilica Ulpia we can still admire **Trajan's Column**, dedicated to M. Ulpius Traianus and commemorating his victorious expeditions against the Dacians (it is 40 m high excluding the basement). Tommaso della Porta's bronze statue of St. Peter has stood on top of the column since 1587. The shaft of the column, consisting of 18 superimposed blocks of marble, is decorated with a continuous spiral frieze immortalizing, in wonderful reliefs, the emperor's victorious campaigns in Dacia. The basement of the column houses the sepulchral chamber in which the emperor wished his ashes to be preserved. Adjacent to the column are the much-depleted ruins of the Basilica Ulpia, but the remains of the columns attest to the grandeur of its architectural plan, consisting of five aisles.

To the rear of the Forum of Trajan is the imposing hemicycle of the **Markets of Trajan**, a commercial complex consisting of three levels of shops; a large hall was also used as a market. Continuing along the Via dei Fori Imperiali, we now come to the **Forum of Augustus**. It was erected to commemorate the victorious battle of Philippi, fought by Augustus in 42 A.D.: the battle in which Brutus and Cassius, the assassins of Caesar, met their death. Of the Temple of Mars Ultor (the god of war to whom the whole Forum was dedicated) some magnificent fluted columns and the frontal stairway remain. Also identifiable are the meagre ruins of the two basilicas and a few other architectural features which formed part of the Forum. Next to the Forum of Augustus is the **Forum of Nerva** (97 A.D.), also called the Forum Transitorium because it provided transit between the popular district of the Suburra, the Roman Forum and the other Forums. Within it stood the Temple of Minerva, whose basement podium remains at the centre of the Forum.

Other remains, at its further end, consist of two half-buried Corinthian columns (known as the **Colonnacce**).

There follows the **Forum of Peace** or **Forum of Vespasian**, of

Julius Caesar

which little remains other than an exedra and some prostrate fragments of column (in front). The **church of Saints Cosmas and Damian** was built over the ruins of a hall forming part of the Forum.

On the other side of the Via dei Fori Imperiali, immediately after the Victor Emanuel Monument, is the **Forum of Caesar**, in front of which stands an imposing bronze statue of Julius Caesar. At the centre of the large piazza of the Forum the emperor erected the **Temple of Venus Genitrix**, whom the Julian clan claimed as ancestress. Other remains form part of the **Basilica Argentaria**.

We now make our way along the Via dei Fori Imperiali to the church of Saints Cosmas and Damian (on the right), which was erected over a hall of the large Forum of Peace in 527. Its interior is in the baroque style, but is notable for its wonderful 6th century mosaics in the apse.

Next to it are the impressive ruins of the **Basilica of Maxentius**, begun by Maxentius in 306 and completed by Constantine in 312, consisting of the nave to the right, the vaulted central nave and one of the two apses. The basilica consisted of three vast arcaded bays: the central one with cross-vaults and the lateral ones with barrel vaults and coffered ceilings.

Adjacent to it stands the **church of Santa Francesca Romana** or **Santa Maria Nova**, dating to the 10th century, but entirely reconstructed in the 13th. In the centuries that followed the church underwent other alterations, including its white travertine façade designed by Carlo Lambardi in the 17th century.

The Forum of Trajan - General views

It is flanked by the Romanesque bell-tower (12th century). The interior, consisting of a single nave, has a fine coffered ceiling (17th century) and a marble-inlaid Cosmatesque floor (13th century). **The mosaic** in the apse dates to 1160. In the sacristy is a 5th century icon of the Virgin: the so-called «Madonna del Conforto».

In the adjacent convent is housed the **Antiquarium Forense**: a small museum elucidating the history of the Roman Forums and consisting of various archaeological material found during the excavations of the Palatine and the Roman Forum. Beyond Santa Francesca Romana extends the huge double **Temple of Venus and Rome**, designed and built by the emperor Hadrian in 135. It was later (307) restored by Maxentius. The temple consisted of two apses: one (dedicated to the goddess Roma) facing towards the Forum, the other (dedicated to Venus) towards the Colosseum.

At the end of the Via dei Fori Imperiali is the Colosseum.

Plastic model of the ancient Rome - The Colosseum

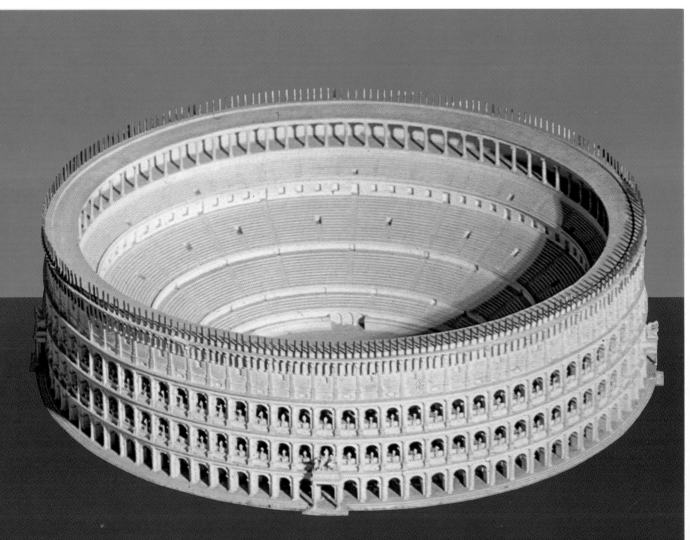

The Colosseum

This is the term commonly used to indicate the Flavian Amphitheatre; it perhaps derives from the fact that a gigantic statue of Nero known as the Colossus was situated adjacent to it. Begun by Vespasian in 72, the Colosseum was completed by his son Titus in the year 80: Titus set aside 100 days of festivity to celebrate its inauguration. It could contain up to 50,000 spectators, who gathered there to watch the famous games which were often cruel, but which aroused enormous enthusiasm in the spectators. The shows staged in the Colosseum included contests between gladiators (in general, specially trained slaves), the hunting of and battles between wild animals (brought to Rome frome the farthest outposts of the Empire), and naval engagement or *naumachiae* (mock sea-fights), to simulate which the arena was flooded with water. The Colosseum was also the place of martyrdom of many early Christians. It goes without saying that, in the building of the Colosseum, the Romans gave proof of all their technical skills and incredible inventiveness. For instance, a system was devised to protect the spectators both from the rain and the heat by a system of awnings overhead (the « Velarium »), the fixtures to support which are still visible in the upper walls.

The Amphitheatre, literally a « double theatre », was so called because it derives from the fusion of two theatres which in ancient Greece consisted of a semicircular series of tiered seats rising from a central orchestra and stage. The result was the creation of an enormous elliptical ring of marble-veneered travertine, rising in four storeys, of which the first three presented arcades with half-columns respectively of the Doric, Ionic and Corinthian orders between them. The top storey, more compact and decorated with Corinthian pilaster strips, was pierced by windows. What we see of the Colosseum today is what remains of this mighty edifice after the depredations of nature (it has been damaged by various earthquakes) and of man, who has not hesitated to use it as a quarry for building materials, and to strip it of marbles and other precious decorations.

The speedy entry and exit of spectators was ensured by the placing of the eighty entrances right round the ground-floor arcades, each of them numbered to indicate the staircases leading to the various sectors of the tiered seating, each of them reserved for a particular category or class: the first for the emperor and the Vestals, and so on right up to the topmost gallery where the common people and women sat. The arena, whose floor has been removed, reveals a complex underground system, which included the various mechanisms and apparatus for the games, and the corridors for the transit of the gladiators and the wild beasts.

The site of the Colossus of Nero, at the end of the Via dei Fori Imperiali, is marked by some travertine slabs set into the road; the gilt bronze statue is thought to have been some c. 30 m. high.

Near to it is the **Arch of Constantine**, a magnificent triple-arcaded triumphal arch raised by the people and the Senate in 312 to celebrate Constantine's victory over Maxentius in the battle of the Milvian Bridge. Composite in its decoration, the arch incorporates medallions and reliefs spoliated from earlier imperial monuments. Its state of conservation is excellent.

In front of the Arch of Constantine was the **Meta Sudans**, a conical brick fountain built by Titus at the end of the 1st century A.D. According to tradition, the gladiators washed and quenched their thirst at this fountain after their contests in the Colosseum. Only the foundations now remain.

Behind the Colosseum rises the Oppian, one of the three heights of the Esquiline, another of the seven hills of Rome. A park now extends over it, incorporating various Roman ruins, including the remains — largely underground — of the **Domus Aurea**. This sumptuously decorated building was the palace of the emperor Nero. On his death, it was covered over, half a century later, by the Baths of Trajan. But of the Domus Aurea it is still possible to admire its long corridors and splendidly frescoed rooms: their discovery and exploration was a source of inspiration to many Renaissance artists.

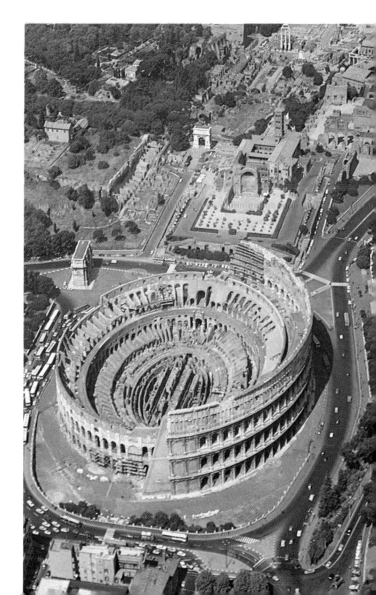

The Colosseum

A view of the interior of the Colosseum ➤

Arch of Constantine

Arch of Constantine (Reconstruction)

Again starting out from the Piazza Venezia, this time we take the road to the right of the Victor Emanuel Monument: the Via del Teatro Marcello. We then turn off to the right into the Piazza Campitelli, on which stands the **church of Santa Maria in Campitelli**, built in the baroque style by Rainaldi in the 17th century. The tabernacle built into the high altar contains an enamelled icon of the Virgin Mary known as the «Madonna in Portico» dating to the 11th century, to whom the cessation of a plague epidemic in 1656 was attributed, and in honour of whom the church as a result was built.

Close by, in the Via dei Funari, is the **church of Santa Caterina dei Funari**, dating back to the 12th century, but reconstructed in the 16th. The splendid façade by Guidetto Guidetti also dates to the 16th century.

On the same street is the huge **Palazzo Mattei di Giove**, built by Maderno towards the end of the 16th century. At its end is the Piazza Mattei, dominated by its charming Renaissance **Fountain of the Tortoises**. Designed by Giacomo Della Porta, the fountain consists of bronze ephebes supporting tortoises, though these were added in the 17th century; the bronze figures are by Taddeo Landini.

We return to the Via del Teatro Marcello. A short distance ahead, to the right, is the **Theatre of Marcellus**. It was actual-

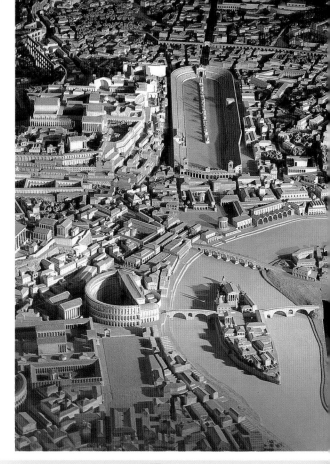

Plastic model of the ancient Rome - Detail with the Tiberina Island, the Circus Maximus and the theatre of Marcellus

Theatre of Marcellus

The Fountain of the Turtles

The Synagogue

ly built by Augustus in the 1st century B.C. in honour of his young nephew Marcellus, whom he intended as his successor but who was cut off by an early death. The Theatre is partly occupied by the Palazzo Orsini, but some of the two series of superimposed tiers of arches that composed it are still visible. Adjacent to it stand three graceful Corinthian columns: all that remain of the **Temple of Apollo Sosiano** erected in 433-31 B.C. The Theatre abuts onto the Piazza di Monte Savello, on which also stands the **church of San Nicola in Carcere**, built over the ruins of three temples, as is clearly attested by the remains of ancient columns incorporated into its walls. The 16th century façade is by Della Porta who made various alterations to the

original building dating to the 11th century.

The stretch of the Tiber facing the piazza on which the church stands is that in which the **Isola Tiberina** lies, the island sacred in ancient times to the god of medicine Aesculapius, to whom a temple was dedicated. The island's medical associations live on in the **Hospital of the Fatebenefratelli** which is now situated on it (founded in the 16th century). Adjacent to it is the **church of San Giovanni Calibita** of the 17th century, while on the other side of the little piazza is the **church of San Bartolomeo** built by the emperor Otto III over the ruins of the Temple of Aesculapius.

The Tiber island is joined to the banks of the river by two Roman bridges. We recross the Pons Fabricius, in the direction whence we came, and make our way to the nearby **Porticus of Octavia**, built in 146 B.C. and reconstructed by Augustus in honour of his sister. Only some columns, part of the entablature and an arch survive of it: they form an entrance to the church of **Sant'Angelo in Peschiera**, which derives its name from the fish-market once situated here. The whole surrounding area is the characteristic Jewish quarter in Rome: the **Ghetto**.

We now return to the Theatre of Marcellus. Continuing our way along the Via del Teatro Marcello, we pass the medieval **House of the Crescenzi**, incorporating Roman reliefs and other ancient architectural fragments in its structure, and so come to the Piazza della Bocca della Verità. It marks the site of the ancient Forum Boarium.

The remains of two ancient temples still stand in the piazza. The rectangular one is the so-called **Temple of Fortuna Virilis**, dating to the 2nd century B.C., and built in an Italo-Greek style which represents a fusion of Hellenistic and Etruscan fea-

The Mouth of Truth

Church of Santa Maria in Cosmedin

tures. Adjacent to it is the graceful **Temple of Vesta**. In structure and circular plan it is of Greek derivation; but the Romans saw in this a reflection of the form of the primitive huts familiar to them. The temple consists of a circular peristyle of Corinthian columns which originally supported an entablature of which no trace remains. It was not in fact dedicated to Vesta: only its circular plan inspired this name.

On the other side of the piazza stands the **church of Santa Maria in Cosmedin**, erected over the remains of Roman buildings in the 6th century and subsequently enlarged and transformed. Its tall and beautiful bell-tower pierced by two- and three-light mullioned windows is in the Romanesque style (12th century). In the portico of the church is preserved a large circular stone mask: this is the famous «**Bocca della Verità**» (mouth of truth) from which the piazza takes its name. The name derives from the legend that if a witness whose truthfulness was doubted placed his hand in the mouth of the mask, it would bite him if he were guilty of telling a lie.

Not far away, at the centre of the Via del Velabro, is the **Arch of Janus**, dating to the period of the emperor Constantine. It has four equal sides, with arches opening to the four points of the compass. Close to it stands the **church of San Giorgio in Velabro**, dating to the 6th century but subjected to various alterations since then. It is flanked by a graceful Romanesque bell-tower (12th century). The interior is in basilica form. The apse is decorated with frescoes dating to 1295, perhaps the work of Pietro Cavallini. Of considerable artistic interest is also the Cosmatesque baldacchino.

Adjacent to the church is the **Arcus Argentarius**, raised in 204 and dedicated to the emperor Septimius Severus, his wife Julia Domna and his sons Caracalla and Geta.

Close to the arch is the drainage channel of the **Cloaca Maxima**, which debouches into the Tiber at this point: this daring work of hydraulic engineering, perhaps dating back to the period of Tarquinius Priscus, was used to drain the once marshy ground of the Forum.

We now make our way towards the Circus Maximus, which still preserves the shape of ancient Rome's chariot-racing track, and, by way of the Via del Circo Massimo, ascend the **Aventine**, another of the hills of Rome, its slopes dotted with secluded villas and laid out with little parks and gardens. Some ancient remains are also to be seen on the hill: a stretch of the Republican walls of Rome and some buildings dating to the

The Temple of Vesta

time of Augustus. The Piazzale Romolo e Remo is dominated by a monument to Giuseppe Mazzini (1949).

On ascending the Aventine, we come to the **church of Santa Sabina**, on the Piazza d'Illiria. Dating back to the 5th century, it still retains, in spite of the numerous alterations to which it has been subject over the centuries, the most characteristic features of an Early Christian basilica. A large 5th century mosaic is preserved above the main portal. The interior is divided into a nave and two aisles by 24 fluted Corinthian columns. On the same road, a little further on, we come to the **church of Santi Bonifacio e Alessio**, founded in the 10th century, but reconstructed by Tommaso De Marchis in the 18th.

In the Piazza dei Cavalieri di Malta is the **Villa of the Knights of Malta**, with its famous keyhole view of St. Peter's, and the **church of Santa Maria del Priorato**. After passing the Piazza Sant'Anselmo, we now descend the street of the same name and so reach the Piazza Albania. Close to the piazza is the **church of San Saba** (7th century) with a Romanesque façade.

We now continue down to the nearby **Porta San Paolo**, one of the Roman gateways in the Aurelian Walls (the Porta Ostiensis), which leads to the basilica of St. Paul Outside the Walls. To the right is the **Pyramid of Caius Cestius**: a Roman tomb with a burial chamber inside, the tomb of Caius Cestius Epulones. Next to it is the **Protestant Cemetery**, running parallel to the Aurelian Walls, where the English Romantic poets Keats and Shelley, the son of Goethe, and many other famous foreign poets and men of letters are buried.

Leaving Rome through the Porta San Paolo, we take the Via Ostiense (2 km.) to St. Paul's, passing, just before we reach it, a Roman cemetery known as the **Sepolcreto Ostiense**. The **Basilica of St. Paul Outside the Walls** is the largest church in the city after St. Peter's. In July 1823 it was almost completely destroyed, together with its inestimable artistic treasures, by a fire. It was rebuilt in 1823-29. The façade, decorated with large mosaics, is preceded by a large four-sided arcade (G. Sacconi). The interior, vast and majestic, consists of a nave and four aisles delimited by 80 huge monolithic columns. The basilica contains a number of precious works of art: the Triumphal Arch separating the transept from the nave with 5th century mosaics; the 13th century Ciborium or Canopy by Arnolfo di Cambio, saved from the fire; the 13th century mosaic in the apse representing Christ and the Apostles; the wonderful 12th century Paschal Candlestick (in the Cosmatesque style, by Vassalletto); and the Chapel of the Crucifix with frescoes by Maderno.

Another wonderful masterpiece annexed to the basilica is its superb early 13th century Cloister, again the work of the Vassalletto family.

Basilica of St. Paul outside the Walls

Basilica of St. Paul outside the Walls - Interior

Basilica of St. Paul outside the Walls - The Cloister

E.U.R.

We now turn into the Via Laurentina, which together with the Via dell'Oceano Atlantico, the Via dell'Oceano Pacifico, the Via Ostiense and the Via delle Tre Fontane, encircles the area (420 hectares) occupied by the **E.U.R.** district.

First we come to the **Abbey of the Tre Fontane**, founded, according to legend, on the site where St. Paul was decapitated. This monastic complex comprises three churches: **Santi Vincenzo ed Anastasio, Santa Maria Scala Coeli**, and **San Paolo alle Tre Fontane**. Facing the Abbey is a sanctuary visited by thousands of pilgrims each year.

We now visit the E.U.R. (the initials stand for « Esposizione Universale di Roma »), the modern district designed as an exhibition centre, but unfortunately abandoned and forgotten due to the Second World War. Only in 1950 did restoration work begin, completed ten years later on the occasion of the Olympic Games in Rome. The district contains a number of public buildings: the **Palazzo dello Sport**, which can contain up to 16,000 spectators, the **Velodrome**, situated in the Viale dei Primati Sportivi, the church of **Saints Peter and Paul**, the **Palazzo della Civiltà del Lavoro**, and the **Palazzo dei Congressi**. The central Piazza Marconi is the site of some interesting museums, such as the **National Museum of Popular Arts and Traditions**, and the **Luigi Pigorini Prehistoric and Ethographic Museum**. The former contains a fascinating collection of popular goldsmith's work and various other artefacts testifying to the customs and traditions of Italian popular life in the early years of the present century. The other museum is also of considerable interest. It is divided into two sections: the first Ethnographic, consisting of three rooms containing a marvellous display of African ritual objects and other artefacts of ethnographic type; and the second Prehistoric, with exhibits illustrating the various prehistoric cultures of Italy.

Also worth visiting is the **Museum of Roman Civilization** (Museo della Civiltà Romana) in the Piazza Agnelli, comprising a large series of plaster-casts and reproductions vividly illustrating the history of Rome from its origins to the 6th century.

E.U.R. - View of the Lake and the Skyscraper   **E.U.R. - Piazza Marconi**

From the Colosseum, by the Via San Gregorio and the Via S. Clivo di Scauro, we reach the **church of Santi Giovanni e Paolo**, very ancient in origin but almost completely restored from the Middle Ages to modern times. Continuing, we cross over the Piazza Navicella and turn into the Via S. Stefano Rotondo, where we find the **church of Santo Stefano Rotondo**, with its characteristic circular form. Erected in the 5th century, it contains a precious mosaic representing Christ superimposed (but not crucified) on the cross. The frescoes along the walls, depicting scenes of martyrdom, are by Pomarancio and Tempesta (16th century). We return to the Piazza S. Gregorio, where the church of the same name stands; it dates back to the 6th century, but has been completely transformed in the course of the centuries.

And so we reach the area once used for chariot races and mock battles in ancient Rome: the **Circus Maximus** (2nd century B.C.). In its environs is the **Porta Capena**, one of the ancient gateways into the city, and, just beyond it, the **church of Santa Balbina** (5th century). The latter contains a Cosmatesque episcopal throne and other medieval fragments.

The church overlooks the famous **Baths of Caracalla**. This vast architectural complex, built by the emperor Caracalla in the 3rd century A.D., consisted of a series of large halls and is still surrounded by delightful gardens. It contained the various component parts of Roman public baths: the Frigidarium, with its large basin; the Tepidarium and the Calidarium, above which was a large dome, as well as gymnasia, libraries and massage-parlours.

On leaving the Baths we visit the **church of San Cesareo in Palatio**, situated on the Via di Porta San Sebastiano. Of very ancient origins, the church was restored by Giacomo Della Porta in the 16th century. The simple interior contains some Cosmatesque features and a fine mosaic in the apse representing God the Father between two angels, by Francesco Zucchi.

Continuing along the same road, we come (on the left) to the **Tomb of the Scipios**, a small catacomb hewn in the soft volcanic rock in which the bodies of the noble Roman family, the Scipios, were interred. At the end of the road, we come to the **Porta San Sebastiano**, a gateway in the Aurelian Walls more commonly known as the Porta Appia, beyond which the so-called « road of the catacombs » begins: the **Via Appia Antica**. It is along this road in fact that we find the labyrinths of passageways dug into the soft volcanic rock and used, in origin, to house the mortal remains of the Christian martyrs, who were buried in little chambers, while the members of Christian families were buried in simple horizontal niches dug into the walls of the galleries. Later the catacombs served as a refuge for Christians, who hid here to escape persecution, and to pray and meet together. A movement of egalitarian spirit like Christianity could not in fact coexist with the society of the day, based on discrimination between slaves and Roman citizens.

The Bath of Caracalla

Ancient Appian way

The Tomb of Cecilia Metella

We now begin to explore what is in fact the oldest road of the city, opened up to provide a road link between Rome and Southern Italy.

Close to an intersection (where the Via Ardeatina branches to the right) we come to the **church of Domine Quo Vadis?** It derives its name from the question that St. Peter, on his escape from the Mamertine prison, reputedly put to Christ, whom he met as he fled along the Appian Way: «Lord, where are you going?». To which the Lord replied: «I am going to Rome to be crucified a second time».

We continue along the Via Appia Antica, turning off to our right to visit the **Catacombs of St. Callixtus**; official burial place of the bishops of Rome, they are named after Pope Callixtus who enlarged and reorganized them in the 3rd century. Other catacombs are situated in this area. On the Via Ardeatina are the **Fosse Ardeatine**, in which the Gemans massacred 355 Italians during the last war; a memorial marks the spot where they are buried. In the nearby Via delle Sette Chiese are the

Catacombs of Domitilla. They are named after Domitilla, the Christian wife of Flavius Clemens (of the imperial Flavian family), to whom the sepulchre above which they were laid out belonged.

We now return to the Via Appia Antica to visit the **Catacombs and church of San Sebastiano**. The former are laid out on four superimposed levels and contain a bust of the Saint attributed to Bernini. The interior of the church, remodelled in the 17th century, contains the Chapel of the Relics, and the Albani and St. Sebastian Chapels.

On the other side of the Via Appia Antica are the **Jewish Catacombs** and the **Catacombs of Praetextatus**. In the latter both pagan and Christian sarcophagi are found.

A short distance ahead, to the left of the Via Appia Antica, are, first, the **Circus of Maxentius**, built in 308, and then the **Tomb of Cecilia Metella**. The latter is the best preserved of the mausolea flanking the Appian Way. It is dedicated to Cecilia Metella, the wife of Crassus (68 B.C.).

Catacombs of St. Calixtus - Crypt of St. Cecilia   **Catacombs of St. Calixtus**

Catacombs of St. Sebastian   **Catacombs of Domitilla**

The Church of San Pietro in Vincoli

From the Piazza Venezia we turn into the Via dei Fori Imperiali, and then turn left into the Via Cavour, so reaching the Piazza San Pietro in Vincoli. It takes its name from the **church of San Pietro in Vincoli**, founded by the wife of the emperor Valentinian III, Eudoxia, who wanted it to be a place of veneration of the holy relic after which it is named: the chains that fettered St. Peter in prison.

In fact, the church's origins are very ancient, even dating back earlier than the 4th century, but its ancient appearance has been substantially altered, notably in its interior, by successive alterations, including the 18th century restoration of Francesco Fontana. The nave, divided from the aisles by ancient fluted columns, still retains something of its original appearance; it is topped by a wooden coffered ceiling which creates a fine scenographic effect; worth noting is Parodi's fresco of « The Miracle of the Chains » with which it is decorated. Apart from various works of art by distinguished artists like Guercino,

Domenichino and Andrea Bregno, the church contains the **Mausoleum of Julius II by Michelangelo**. According to the artist's design, the monument, begun on the commission of Pope Julius II in 1513, was intended to be enormously grander and more imposing in the number and size of its sculptures than what we see today. But, at the behest of Leo X, Michelangelo was later obliged to curtail his work on the project. What remains is the wonderful statue of **Moses** at its centre. This is a masterpiece of sculpture. The virile figure of the biblical patriarch, seated on a throne, and admonishing the idolatrous Jews with a penetrating and indignant eye, makes a powerful impression.

From San Pietro in Vincoli we ascend the Esquiline Hill, where we find the **church of San Martino ai Monti** in the piazza of the same name. Its origins can be traced back to the 14th century, but it was remodelled in the 17th.

Church of San Pietro in Vincoli - Interior   **Church of San Pietro in Vincoli - The Moses of Michelangelo**

The Basilica of St. Mary Major

By way of the Via Quattro Cantoni and then the Via Paolina, we reach the **Basilica of St. Mary Major**, one of the major Early Christian basilicas of Rome. According to tradition, it was built by Pope Liberius on the place where, after the apparition of the Virgin, snow had fallen in the middle of summer. The 18th century façade by Ferdinando Fuga consists of an elegant triple-arcaded loggia, behind which are some late 13th century mosaics representing the above-cited miracle. The interior, with a nave and two aisles divided by splendid monolithic Ionic columns, is striking for its beauty and solemnity, thanks also to the sumptuous gilt coffered ceiling over the nave, perhaps the work of Giuliano Sangallo. Noteworthy too is the Cosmatesque floor (12th century). Above the entablature are some precious 5th century mosaics representing scenes from the Old Testament. In the apse is Iacopo Torriti's splendid mosaic of the « Triumph of Mary ». The basilica contains a fine 18th century baldacchino over the high alter by Fuga and a number of important chapels:
— the Sistine Chapel, built for Sixtus V by Domenico Fontana in the later 16th century and frescoed by a group of Mannerist painters; it contains a gilt ciborium in the shape of a small circular temple by Ludovico Scalzo;
— the Pauline (or Borghese) Chapel, built for Paul V by Flaminio Ponzio in the 17th century; it contains frescoes by Guido Reni;
— the Sforza Chapel, built by Giacomo della Porta after a design by Michelangelo.
The Basilica is flanked by a fine Romanesque bell-tower: the highest in Rome (75 m.). From the Piazza Santa Maria Maggiore we continue along the Via Merulana, making a short detour a short distance ahead to the right to visit **the church of Santa Prassede**. Erected in the 5th century, it was completely rebuilt in the 9th and, in the course of the ensuing centuries, has undergone various alterations and enlargements. It contains some splendid mosaics of the 9th century. The Chapel of St. Zeno, an important monument of the Byzantine period in Rome, also dates to this period. The bones of St. Praxed and her sister St. Pudentiana, early converts to Christianity, and many other Christian relics, are preserved in this church. Before continuing our itinerary, let us make another detour,

Basilica of St. Mary Major

Basilica of St. Mary Major - Interior

Basilica of St. Mary Major - Mosaic of the Apsis

making our way round to the back of the Basilica of St. Mary Major (Piazza dell'Esquilino) to visit the **church of Santa Pudenziana** of very ancient origins, but recently transformed; some rémains of the original building are still preserved in its interior.

We now take the Via Carlo Alberto, noting (to the left) the **church of Sant'Antonio** and the **Arch of Gallienus**. The street leads into the large arcaded Piazza Vittorio Emanuele II, from where, by way of the Via Mamiani, we reach the long thoroughfare, the Via Giolitti, one end of which ends at the Railway Station (**Stazione Termini**) and the Piazza dei Cinquecento facing it, and the other at the Piazza di Porta Maggiore. We cross over the station (by the Via S. Bibiana) to visit the **Basilica of St. Laurence Outside the Walls**. The church owes its origins to Constantine who wanted to build a sacred shrine over the site where St. Laurence had been martyred. Later Pope Sixtus III decided to erect another one close to the first. Later still, in the 8th century, the two buildings were joined together into a single basilica. Worth noting in the interior are the medieval episcopal throne, canopy and two pulpits.

A few steps from the Basilica is the **Cemetery of Campo Verano**, the city's major burial place where many celebrated personalities are buried.

From the Piazza San Lorenzo where the second highest column in Rome stands (after that of the Immaculata in the Piazza di Spagna), we can take the Via Cesare De Lollis to visit the **University City**: this extensive campus contains some interesting museums, including the **Museum of Origins,** with exhibits relating to various geological eras, and the **Museum of Mineralogy.**

Following the Via dei Fori Imperiali (again starting out from the Piazza Venezia), and circling the Colosseum, we reach the Via San Giovanni in Laterano on which the **church of San Clemente** is situated. The basilica in fact consists of two superimposed churches: the upper one with a fine baroque façade by Fontana and a lower one (4th century), interred below ground to permit the construction of the later church built over it (12th century). The interior of the upper church, remodelled in the 17th century, has a nave and two aisles divided by ancient columns. It contains a 12th century « schola cantorum »; a 12th century mosaic of the « Triumph of the Cross » in the apse; and 15th century frescoes by Masolino da Panicale in the Chapel of St. Catherine of Alexandria. From the sacristy we descend to the lower basilica which retains a series of valuable frescoes.

Nearby, at the beginning of the Via dei Quattro Santi Coronati, is the church of the same name, dating back to the 4th century but variously transformed. Of particular interest is its fine early 13th century Cloister. The church itself preserves its ancient granite columns and Cosmatesque floor. Below is a Crypt where the relics of some martyr saints are preserved.

We continue to the Piazza San Giovanni in Laterano, at the centre of which stands the **Egyptian Obelisk**, the tallest of the thirteen obelisks extant in Rome. Brought here from the Circus Maximus in 1588, it dates to the 15th century B.C. To its right is the **Lateran Baptistery**, which has ancient origins; it was erected by Constantine. At the centre of its polygonal interior is a large font in green basalt in which the sacrament of baptism was administered by immersion. It is surrounded by a colonnade of porphyry columns supporting a cornice with smaller white marble columns above, and four chapels with wonderful mosaics dating from the 5th and 7th centuries.

The Basilica of St. John Lateran

We now visit the **Basilica of St. John Lateran**, second only to St. Peter's in importance. It was erected at the beginning of the 4th century over an area of the family palace of the Laterani donated to the church by the emperor Constantine. Damaged by fires and earthquakes, sacked during the barbarian invasions, the basilica has been continuously reconstructed, enlarged and enriched with precious decorations and works of art. It was extensively remodelled in the baroque style by Borromini in the 17th century. Its main façade was raised in the 18th century by Alessandro Galilei: simple and yet majestic, it consists of a single order of huge pilasters supporting a ponderous entablature with a balustrade above, topped, against the skyline, by 15 statues of Christ and flanking saints. Below is the portico, providing access to the five entrances to the basilica. The middle one has Roman bronze doors brought from the Curia in the Roman Forum; the one to the far right is the Porta Santa.

The huge interior is divided into a nave and four aisles. The nave is topped by a sumptuous gilt wooden ceiling (16th century), and has a fine Cosmatesque floor. Large niches containing statues of the 12 Apostles are placed between the piers of the nave. Among the treasures contained in the basilica, we may cite: the magnificent tabernacle placed over the papal altar sculpted in the gothic style by Giovanni di Stefano in the 14th century and enshrining the heads of Saints Peter and Paul; the delicately carved bronze tomb-slab of Martin V; the transept restored by Giacomo Della Porta, decorated with frescoes which are genuine masterpieces of 16th century art; the apse with 13th century mosaics by Jacopo Turriti and Jacopo da Camerino; and, in the left aisle, the elegant Corsini Chapel designed by Alessandro Galilei (1734). On the first pillar to the left in the intermediate aisle to the right is a fragmentary fresco of « Boniface VIII proclaiming the Jubilee in 1300 » attributed to Giotto. At the foot of the aisle to the far left is the door leading into the beautiful Cosmatesque Cloister, the work of the Vassalletto family.

On the right flank of the basilica is the **Lateran Palace**. Pope Sixtus V commissioned the architect Domenico Fontana in 1586 to totally reconstruct it over the ruins of the former papal palace — the gift of Constantine — with the intention of establishing the summer residence of the Popes in it; an aim that was never realized. The palace previously housed the Lateran Museums, comprising the Christian, Profane and Missionary Ethnological collections, which have now been transferred to the Vatican. The interior, recently restored, is richly frescoed (the painters involved in its decoration included Baldassarre Croce, Cesare Nebbia and Giovanni Battista Ricci). In a building on the other side of the piazza is the **Scala Santa**: the staircase which, according to tradition, was ascended by Christ on his way to be judged by Pontius Pilate. The building was erected by Domenico Fontana for Sixtus V in the 16th century as a fitting setting to house the **Chapel of St. Laurence**: the papal chapel. Richly decorated with works of art, the chapel contains Christian relics of great value. For this reason it is known

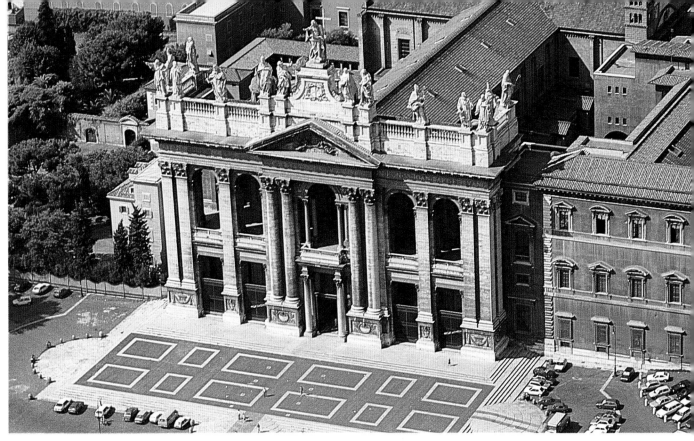

Basilica of St. John Lateran

Basilica of St. John Lateran - Interior

as the **Sancta Sanctorum**. Over the altar is a portrait of Jesus Christ, which is invested with peculiar sanctity, because it is thought to have been begun by St. Luke and finished by an angel: hence the name by which it is known, **Acheiropoëton**, or 'picture made without hands'.

In the piazza facing the main façade of St. John Lateran is a **Monument to Francis of Assisi**.

The adjacent Porta San Giovanni, one of the gateways in the Aurelian Walls, marks the starting point of the Via Appia Nuovo, by means of which we can reach the famous little towns in the Alban Hills known as the Castelli Romani (Castelgandolfo, summer residence of the Pope; Marino and Frascati, famous for their wines).

From the Piazza San Giovanni in Laterano we now take the Viale Carlo Felice to the Piazza Santa Croce in Gerusalemme on which the **Basilica of Santa Croce in Gerusalemme** stands. Dating back as early as the 4th century, it was completely remodelled in the baroque period. It contains the relic of the Cross of Jesus Christ (hence its name). A short distance away is the Piazza Porta Maggiore where we find one of the most impressive Roman gateways of the city, the **Porta Maggiore** (erected by the emperor Claudius to carry the Claudian Aqueduct in 52 A.D.). Here too, on the same piazza, is the **Basilica** of the same name, an underground sanctuary which was only discovered in 1917. It can be dated to the early years of the 1st century A.D. It contains a number of notable mythological wall paintings. We can conclude our itinerary by visiting the **Catacombs of Marcellinus and Petrus**, which can be reached by way of the Via Casilina, which starts out from outside the Porta Maggiore.

Again taking the Piazza Venezia as our departure point, we can visit the nearby **Palazzo Colonna** (reachable by way of the Via C. Battisti, the Via IV Novembre, and then turning left into the Via della Pilotta). Residence of the Colonna family, it was built by Martin V in the 15th century, but dates, in its present form, to the 18th century. The linearity and simplicity of the building's external structure is at variance with the pomp and sumptuousness that characterize its interior. The **Colonna Gallery** housed inside the palace is displayed in three large rooms, and comprises an interesting collection of paintings: «Narcissus», by **Tintoretto**; «Portrait of C. Colonna», by **Van Dyck**; «Apollo and Daphne», by **Poussin**; «Guidobaldo da Montefeltro», by **Melozzo da Forlì**, and others.

Further along the Via IV Novembre we come to the Markets of Trajan, adjacent to which rises the 13th century **Torre delle Milizie**, one of the medieval defensive towers of the city, with the 17th century **church of Santa Caterina** next to it. We continue along the Via Nazionale, one of the main thoroughfares of Rome, always crowded with people. To the left is the exhibition centre, the **Palazzo delle Esposizioni**, built in the 19th century after a design by the architect Pio Piacentini. Next to it is the **church of San Vitale** built in the 5th century, but remodelled in subsequent periods; the portal of the façade, in the 15th century style, bears the coat of arms of Pope Sixtus IV. Further ahead, to the right of the Via Nazionale, is the American protestant **church of St. Paul's,** with a valuable cycle of mosaics inside. In the Via Firenze just after the church is Rome's **Opera House**.

And so we come to the **Piazza Esedra**: a large piazza dominated at its centre by the famous **Fountain of the Naiads**, represent-

The Scala Santa

Chapel of San Lorenzo or Sancta Sanctorum

ing the Nymph of the underground waters, borne on a dragon, the Nymph of the oceans, the Nymph of the rivers, and the Nymph of the lakes with a swan. The central figure is that of Glaucus who dominates the forces of nature.

Situated in the Piazza Esedra is the **church of Santa Maria degli Angeli**. Designed by Michelangelo in the 16th century, it made use of ruins belonging to the nearby Baths of Diocletian (being largely converted from one of the great halls of the Baths). In the 18th century, however, Vanvitelli was called to build the Chapel of St. Nicola Albergati, thus modifying the interior's original appearance as designed by Michelangelo. The church is full of works of art, including the « Punishment of Ananias » by Pomarancio, the « Crucifixion of St. Peter » by Ricciolini, the « Martyrdom of St. Sebastian », by Domenichino, and « The Mass of St. Basil » by P. Subleyras. A number of interesting funerary monuments are also contained in the church, such as those of Cardinals Alciati and Parisi, and those of the artists Salvator Rosa and Carlo Maratta.

The **Baths of Diocletian** house the **Museo Nazionale Romano**. Founded in 1889, the museum contains numerous works of Greek and Roman sculpture, sarcophagi, terracottas and paintings. In the Room of the Masterpieces are displayed the « Diskobolos of Castel Porziano », a copy of Myron's original in bronze, and the « Niobe of the Orti Sallustiani ». The important Ludovisi collection comprises among its 102 sculptures such statues as the « Dying Gaul and his Dead Wife », « Aphrodite » and the « Ludovisi Ares ».

We now make our way back down the Via Nazionale, until we come to the Piazza Magnapoli. Here we turn right into the Via XXIV Maggio, on which the **Villa Colonna** and the **church of San Silvestro al Quirinale** are situated. The latter, erected in the 11th century, was completely transformed in the 16th. Close by is the **Palazzo Rospigliosi Pallavicini**, built in 1603: it contains a famous **Gallery** containing paintings by Caravaggio, Rubens, Botticelli, Raphael and other illustrious artists. Its garden pavillion, the **Casino dell'Aurora**, is decorated with a beautiful ceiling fresco by Guido Reni. We have now arrived in the **Piazza del Quirinale** dominated by its magnificent **Fountain of the Dioscuri**. The **Quirinal Palace** faces onto the piazza. Completed by such distinguished architects as Bernini, Fontana and Maderno in the 17th century, it takes its name from the hill on which it stands: the Quirinal. A monumental portal leads into an arcaded courtyard, at the foot of which is the clock-tower and a mosaic of the Virgin Mary based on a design by Maratta. The sumptuously decorated state-rooms of the palace are adorned with frescoes by Maratta, Guido Reni and other distinguished artists, and hung with 16th and 17th century tapestries.

The palace is now the official residence of the President of the Republic.

Also facing onto the piazza is the **Palazzo della Consulta**, built by the architect Ferdinando Fuga in the 18th century, and now the seat of Italy's Constitutional Court. Further ahead, on the Via Quirinale, is the **church of Sant'Andrea al Quirinale**, a masterpiece of Bernini who built it in 1671. Its interior, elliptical in form, is decorated with beautiful frescoed chapels and polychrome marbles; worth mentioning among the works of art is Borgognone's « Crucifixion of St. Andrew » over the high altar. At the foot of the same street is the **church of San Carlino**, a masterpiece of Borromini. We now turn left into the Via

delle Quattro Fontane, so called on account of the four fountains placed at the corners of the intersection. This brings us into the **Piazza Barberini** with Bernini's graceful **Fountain of the Triton** in the middle. Adjacent to the piazza is the **Palazzo Barberini**, considered among the most sumptuous palaces of the Roman nobility. Erected by Maderno in the 17th century, it was completed by Borromini and Bernini. On opposite sides of the entrance are, to the right, a magnificent spiral staircase by Borromini and, to the left, the grand staircase by Bernini, leading up to the main rooms on the first floor . Here we find the large hall with its famous ceiling fresco of the « Triumph of the Barberini » by Pietro da Cortona. In the past the palace housed the Barberini Gallery and a Library of over 60,000 books, subsequently acquired by the Vatican Library. It now houses the **Galleria Nazionale di Arte Antica**: an important picture gallery which includes paintings by Raphael (« La Fornarina »), Fra Angelico (« Triptych »), Tintoretto and Perugino. At a corner of the Piazza Barberini we find Bernini's charming little **Fountain of the Bees**, which marks the beginning of the elegant **Via Vittorio Veneto**, a fashionable street flanked by luxury hotels, shops and cosmopolitan cafés where it is possible to meet famous people from the world of culture and entertainment. It is agreeable to stroll along the Via Veneto just to savour the fascination of this city and the atmosphere that pervades it.

On the Via Veneto we also find the **church of Santa Maria Concezione** or **church of the Capuchins**, built in the 17th century and containing Guido Reni's altarpiece of « The Archangel St. Michael » and Caravaggio's beautiful « St. Francis ». Close by is the **church of Sant'Isidoro**, while at the point where the Via Veneto bends to the left is the **Palazzo Margherita**, once the residence of Queen Margherita of Savoy and now the American Embassy.

Another fascinating tour through the streets of the city is the one to **Castro Pretorio**, Porta Pia, along the Via Salaria and Nomentana, to the **Villa Torlonia**, bearing in mind the many churches, palaces and piazzas we will encounter along our route.

Our departure point this time is the Piazza Barberini: from here we take the Via Barberini to the Piazza San Bernardo with the two **churches of San Bernardo and Santa Susanna** (17th century).

Continuing along the Via XX Settembre, we can branch off to the right (by the Via Goito) to the **Castro Pretorio** (barracks of the Pretorian Guards), or continue straight to the **Porta Pia** at the end of the street. This impressive gateway, famous for the episode of the taking of Rome in 1870, was designed by Michelangelo and built by Della Porta. We pass through the gate and continue straight on along the Via Nomentana, a wide thoroughfare flanked by rich and famous historic villas: Paganini, Mirafiori, Torlonia, Agnese and, on the Via Salaria, Albani, Chigi and Ada.

The first we come to (on the right) is the **Villa Torlonia**, with its twin obelisks. Built by Valadier in the neo-classic style, and completed by Caretti, it was the property of the affluent banker Torlonia who wanted to create a splendid residence amid a landscape of lawns and tall palm-trees.

Further along the Via Nomentana (to the left) is the **Basilica of St. Agnes Outside the Walls**, built in 342 over the Catacombs in which the mortal remains of the Saint were preserved. Adjacent to it is the **church of Santa Costanza**, an unusual circular Early Christian building, built by Constantine as a mausoleum for his daughters and later converted into a church; it is decorated with beautiful 4th century mosaics. We return to the Porta Pia and, by way of the Corso Italia, reach Piazza Fiume, whence begins the **Via Salaria**. Situated on this major road are the **Villa Chigi**, built for Cardinal F. Chigi; the extensive **Villa Ada**, formerly the property of the House of Savoy, now a public park; and the **Villa Albani**. The latter initially housed a valuable collection of ancient art, later acquired by Alessandro Torlonia together with the villa. The two finest buildings of the complex are the **Casino** and the **Caféhaus**, set amid the beautiful park of pines, cedars and sequoias. The gallery in the Casino contains some interesting paintings by Perugino, Tintoretto, Guercino and others. Also on the Via Salaria are the **Catacombs of Priscilla**, considered the most important in the city. Beyond the Aniene river stretches the modern **Montesacro** quarter.

Starting out once again from the Piazza Venezia, we take the Via C. Battisti, turning left into the Piazza Santi Apostoli in which the **Basilica of the Santi Apostoli** (4th century) is situated. Modernized by Fontana and Valadier in the 18th century, the basilica contains some fine Renaissance tombs, the beautiful Chapel of the Crucifix and other valuable works of art.

From the nearby Piazza della Pilotta, we take the Via San Vincenzo Lucchesi which leads us to the spectacular **Trevi Fountain**. Erected for Clement XII by the architect Nicolò Salvi towards the end of the 17th century, it shows at its centre the statue of Ocean riding in a sea-chariot drawn by two Tritons. Into the basin below, symbolizing the sea, it is the time-honoured custom to throw a coin to guarantee a return to this splendid city. Nearby, in the Palazzo Carpegna, is the **Academy of St. Luke**, which now houses an interesting gallery with paintings by Guido Reni, Guercino, Titian, Van Dyck and others.

We then emerge onto the Via del Tritone, a bustling modern thoroughfare, full of boutiques and crowded with shoppers at all times of the day. Turning off to the left (along the Via Nazareno) we can visit the **church of Sant'Andrea delle Fratte**, flanked by Borromini's graceful brick belfry: it is nicknamed the «campanile ballerino» due to the slight oscillations it registers whenever the bells are rung.

The Fountain of Trevi

The Piazza di Spagna

Elegant and scenic, the Piazza di Spagna provides a welcoming point of encounter at the centre of Rome. Its peculiar fascination derives from a combination of colour, the 18th century buildings that surround it, the flowers that adorn the Spanish Steps, and the animated and cosmopolitan atmosphere that pervades it. From this piazza fan out such prestigious streets as the **Via Margutta**, famous because of the many painters who live and display their works there; the **Via del Babuino**, with its many antique shops; the **Via Condotti**, with its sophisticated boutiques and celebrated **Caffè Greco**, dating back to the 18th century, a historic place of rendezvous of great Italian and foreign artists; the **Via Borgognona**, it too flanked by fashionable boutiques and couturiers; and the lively **Via Frattina**. At the centre of the Piazza di Spagna is placed a marvellous fountain in the shape of a boat: the **Fontana della Barcaccia**, designed by Pietro Bernini, father of the more famous Gian Lorenzo, who was the architect, in part, of the nearby **Palazzo di Propaganda Fide**: he was responsible for the façade looking onto the piazza, while the lateral elevation was by Borromini.

Yet the soul of the piazza consists of the **Spanish Steps** which rise from it. Designed by Francesco De Sanctis in the early years of the 18th century, this elegant staircase ascends in three ramps from the piazza, interrupted by terraces, the last and most scenic of which is the one with the balustrade on top: the Piazza Trinità dei Monti with its obelisk, formerly in the gardens of Sallust on the Quirinal and set up here in 1789. Always thronged with young people, foreigners, musicians and artists selling their wares, the Spanish Steps are enlivened each May by the vivid display of azaleas from the municipal glasshouses. At the top of the Steps is the **church of the Trinità dei Monti**, built in the 16th century on behalf of the French king Louis XII. The handsome façade, by Carlo Maderno, is approached by two converging flights of stairs (designed by Domenico Fontana), and topped by two symmetrical belfries. The church contains some interesting paintings.

We are now on the Pincian Hill. Turning left into the Viale Trinità dei Monti, we soon come (on the right) to the **Villa Medici**. Built in the 16th century, it passed into the hands of France during the Napoleonic period and later became the seat of the **French Academy**, established by Louis XIV for promising young Frenchman wishing to develop their knowledge of art. We now enter the **Pincio**, the magnificent public park laid out by Valadier in the early years of the 19th century. From here we can enjoy marvellous panoramic views over the city, particularly lovely at sunset.

The steps and the church of Trinità dei Monti

Continuing our walk, we enter the extensive gardens of the **Villa Borghese,** full of soaring Roman pines and other trees, extensive lawns, little lakes and fountains. All this makes a wonderful setting for the Villa Borghese itself, which was built for Cardinal Scipione Borghese by Vasanzio between 1613 and 1615. It now houses the **Borghese Museum and Gallery.**

On the groundfloor we may visit the **Borghese Museum** distributed in various rooms, in which some of the greatest masterpieces of Italian sculpture of the 17th and 18th century are displayed, together with statues and marble fragments of antiquity.

In the great hall we find 12 busts of Emperors sculpted by Giovanni Battista Della Porta in the 16th century. In the other rooms: Canova's enchanting **Venus Victrix,** a portrait of Pauline Borghese, the sister of Napoleon and wife of Prince C. Borghese; Gian Lorenzo Bernini's youthful statue of **David with the Sling,** sculpted for Cardinal Scipione Borghese when the artist was only eighteen; the **Apollo and Daphne,** another youthful work by Bernini, the group of **Aeneas and Anchises,** sculpted by Gian Lorenzo in collaboration with his father Pietro Bernini; and the painting of **Saints Cosmas and Damian** by Dosso Dossi.

In the **Gallery of the Emperors,** adorned with 18 busts of emperors dating to the 17th century, is another wonderful sculptural group by Gian Lorenzo Bernini: **The Rape of Proserpine.** The first floor houses the **Borghese Gallery,** which contains a fine collection of paintings by distinguished artists, including Raphael (**Deposition from the Cross**), Caravaggio (**The Madonna dei Palafrenieri**), Titian (**Sacred and Profane Love**), Antonello da Messina (**Portrait of a Man**), Pinturicchio, Botticelli and Rubens.

Leaving the villa in which the Borghese Museum and Gallery are housed, we find, situated close to it, the **Zoological Garden,** founded in 1911, and, on the Via Aldrovandi, the **Civic Museum of Zoology** and the **African Museum.** The latter contains some interesting exhibits illustrating the history and traditions of Africa.

Continuing along the Via Aldrovandi, we come to the Valle Giulia in which the Palazzo delle Belle Arti is situated; it houses the **National Gallery of Modern Art,** founded in 1883.

The gallery contains works by the greatest names in Italian and foreign painting and sculpture of the 19th and 20th century: among the neoclassical artists, **Canova;** among the artists of the Romantic school, **Hayez** and **Segantini;** among the Macchiaioli (Italian impressionists), **Fattori** and **Signorini;** and then **Degas, Monet, Cézanne, Van Gogh, Modigliani, Mafai, De Chirico** and **Guttuso.**

Borghese Museum↗

The Piazza del Popolo

Gallery of the Emperors↘

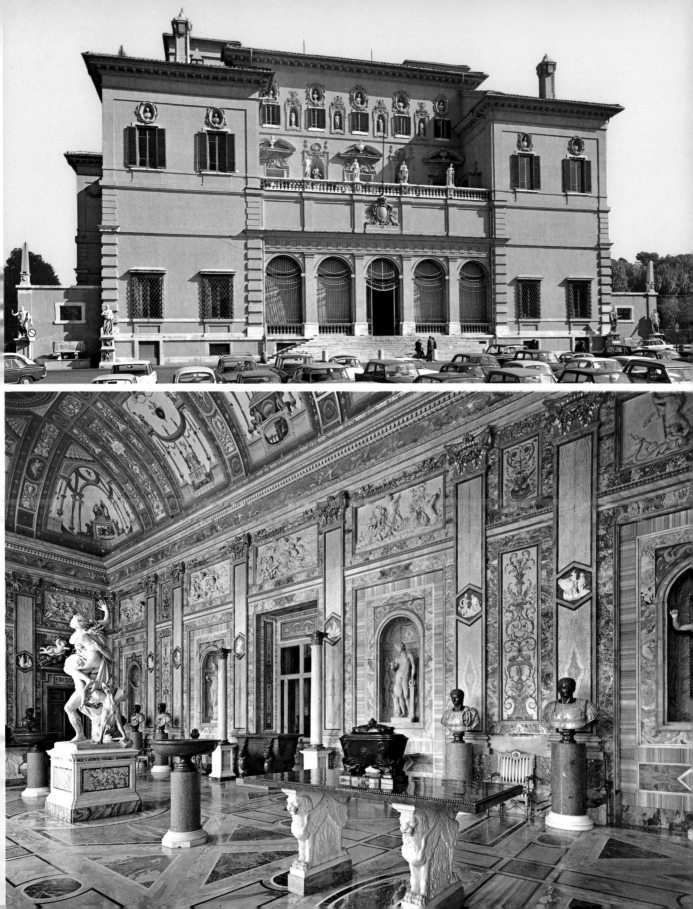

Apollo and Daphne (Bernini)

Aeneas and Anchises (G. Lorenzo and P. Bernini)

Truth (Bernini)

Pauline Borghese Bonaparte (Canova)

David (Bernini)

The Rape of Proserpina (Bernini)

Madonna with Child, St. John and Angels (Botticelli)

**St. John the Baptist in the
Wilderness (Caravaggio)**

Madonna with Child (G. Bellini)

Boy with a Basket of Fruit (Caravaggio)

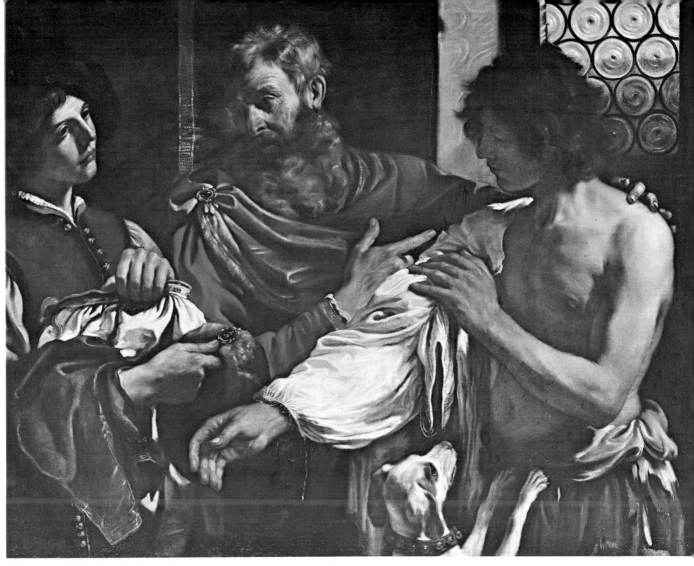

The return of the Prodigal Son (Guercino)

Sacred and Profane Love (Titian)

We now take the Viale delle Belle Arti on which the Villa Giulia — the Villa of Pope Julius III — is situated. It now houses the **National Museum of Villa Giulia**, comprising rich and wideranging collections of archaeological artefacts of the pre-Roman period, notably those of the Etruscans, found during excavations conducted in the territories of Central Italy.

Among the various grave goods, statues and reconstructions of tombs on display, we find the wonderful Etruscan terracotta sculpture of a husband and wife recumbent on a sarcophagus lid: the **Sarcophagus of the «Married Couple»**.

FROM THE CORSO TO THE FORO ITALICO

The Via del Corso is a long straight street linking the Piazza Venezia with the Piazza del Popolo. It is flanked by many imposing palaces built in various periods and in various styles. Starting out once again from the Piazza Venezia, we find, to the left, on the corner of the Corso, the 17th century **Palazzo Bonaparte** (where Napoleon's mother lived). It is followed, on the opposite side of the Corso, by the **Palazzo Salviati**, baroque in style, and the **Palazzo Odescalchi** (19th century). Opposite is the large **Palazzo Doria**, containing the **Doria Pamphilj Gallery**: a magnificent private collection of works of art including such masterpieces as: «Spain succouring Religion» by **Titian**; «Portrait of a Prelate» by **Tintoretto**; «Rest during the Flight into Egypt» and «Mary Magdalen», youthful works by **Caravaggio**; «St. Sebastian» by **Ludovico Carracci**; «Portrait of Innocent X» by **Velazquez**; «Madonna and Child» by

Villa Giulia National Museum - The Apollo of Veii

Villa Giulia National Museum - The Sarcophagus of the Married Couple

Parmigianino; and «Bust of Innocent X» by **Bernini**. Adjacent to the palace is the **church of Santa Maria in Via Lata**, of very ancient origins, but subjected to numerous alterations and restorations during the 11th, 15th and 17th centuries. The existing baroque façade is by Pietro da Cortona. The interior, with a nave and two aisles, is notable for its beautiful high altar adorned with alabaster columns, attributed to Bernini.

On the Via Lata on the corner of the church is a little fountain known as the **Fountain of the Porter**, another of the «speaking statues» of Rome. Continuing along this street we come to the **Collegio Romano** (16th century). The building, designed by Bartolomeo Ammannati, was in the past an important college run by the Jesuits.

The **church of San Marcello**, situated on the Corso, dates back to the early years of the 4th century, but in the 16th century was devastated by a fire which destroyed every trace of the original building. The existing structure is by Iacopo Sansovino, while the baroque façade was designed by Carlo Fontana. Facing it is the **Palace of the Banco di Roma**, an 18th century building by Alessandro Specchi. It is followed by the **Palace of the Cassa di Risparmio** by Antonio Cipolla and, on the opposite side of the Corso, the **Palazzo Sciarra Colonna** (16th century). Nearby is the **church of Sant'Ignazio di Loyola**, reachable by taking the Via Caravita. It was designed by the Jesuit father Orazio Grassi, on the basis of earlier designs by Carlo Maderno. The lavish baroque interior was decorated by Andrea Pozzo, who also frescoed the imposing vault over the nave. By way of the Via dei Burrò we reach the Piazza di Pietra, in which an imposing row of columns is all that remains of the Temple of Hadrian. From here we make our way into the nearby Piazza Colonna, dominated by the Column of Marcus Aurelius, similar in structure to Trajan's Column and erected in 180-196. The Piazza is flanked by the **Palazzo della Galleria Colonna**, the **Palazzo Ferraioli** and the **church of San Bartolomeo del Bergamaschi**, the fountain by **Giacomo Della Porta** (16th century).

At the centre of the adjacent Piazza Montecitorio is the **obelisk of Psammeticus II**, raised here by Pius VI in 1792. Facing it is the **Palazzo Montecitorio**, begun by Bernini in 1650 and completed by Carlo Fontana. The building is now the seat of Italy's Chamber of Deputies.

Returning to the Corso, on the corner of the Piazza Colonna, to our left, is the façade of the **Palazzo Chigi**, a 16th century building which is now the seat of the Prime Minister. Almost facing it, on the corner of the Via del Tritone, is the **church of Santa Maria in Via**, dating back to the 10th century, but its façade by Rainaldi is much later (17th century). The **Caffè Aragno** (now Alemagna) on the Corso is worth mentioning: dating to 1870, it was a famous rendezvous of the intellectual and political élite of the time.

In the Piazza di San Lorenzo in Lucina we can visit the **church of San Lorenzo**, which has very ancient origins: founded in the 4th or 5th century on the site of a Roman house, it was reconstructed in c. 1100, the period to which belong the beautiful Romanesque bell-tower and the portico.

Continuing along the Corso, we see on our left the 16th century **Palazzo Ruspoli** and, just beyond it, the **church of Santi Ambrogio e Carlo al Corso**, built by the architect Onofrio Longhi in the period 1612 to 1672 and completed by his son Martino. But the huge dome was designed by Pietro da Cortona. Having reached the end of the Via del Corso, we finally enter the **Piazza del Popolo**: a wonderfully scenic square laid out by Giuseppe Valadier at the beginning of the 19th century. The piazza opens at the confluence of a «trident» of streets: the Via di Ripetta, the Via del Corso and the Via del Babuino. At its entrance are the two churches of **Santa Maria di Montesanto and Santa Maria dei Miracoli**, erected in the 17th century. After the initial work by Carlo Rainaldi, they were completed by Bernini and Fontana.

Two hemicycles enclose the Piazza, which on one side is flanked by the Pincian Hill.

At its centre is the **Flaminian Obelisk**: carved out of red granite in Egypt in 1232-1200 B.C., it was transported to Rome by Augustus. The fountains and lions at its base are the work of Valadier.

The piazza terminates at the Porta del Popolo. It is flanked by the church of **Santa Maria del Popolo**, which wonderfully completes the scenic ensemble of the square. The church arose over an ancient chapel built, in the late 11th century, at public expense (according to some, it is this fact that gave rise to its name). Following an enlargement in the 13th century, it assumed its present Renaissance appearance in the second half of the 15th. The prolongation of the chancel, with its coffered barrel vault and shell apse, is the work of Bramante.

The interior with a nave and two aisles divided by travertine columns displays the restorations in the baroque style carried out by Bernini.

The church contains works of art of considerable importance: the 1st chapel of the right aisle is decorated with frescoes by Pinturicchio and tombs sculpted by Andrea Bregno, Mino da Fiesole and Francesco da Sangallo. Next to it is the Cybo Chapel by Carlo Fontana with a painting by Carlo Maratto over its altar. Over the High Altar is the venerated icon of the «Madonna del Popolo» (13th century), while behind it, in the chancel, are the funerary monuments of Cardinal Girolamo Basso Della Rovere and Cardinal Ascanio Sforza, the masterpiece of Andrea Sansovino. In the left transept are Caravaggio's two magnificent paintings of the «Conversion of St. Paul» and the «Crucifixion of St. Peter». In the left aisle is the Chigi Chapel designed by Raphael, who also designed the mosaics in the cupola.

Adjacent to the church is the **Porta del Popolo**, at one time the ancient Roman gateway of the Porta Flaminia. It was reconstructed in 1561, based on a design by Michelangelo and Vignola. The façade looking onto the piazza is by Bernini. The Piazzale Flaminio outside the gate is flanked, to the right, by the main entrance to the Villa Borghese, and marks the beginning of the Via Flaminia, the road that ever since antiquity linked Rome with Rimini on the Adriatic. Facing onto the road, on the corner of the Viale delle Belle Arti, is the **Palazzina of Pius IV**, whose design is perhaps attributable in part to Vignola. A short distance further along the Via Flaminia is the **Chapel of Sant'Andrea** by Vignola.

Further on is the **Flaminian Stadium**, erected in 1960 by the architect Nervi on the occasion of the Olympic Games. Other sports grounds and facilities were laid out in the same area. In its environs is the modern residential quarter of **Parioli**. From the Viale dei Parioli we can reach the source of the **Acqua Acetosa**, an excellent mineral water.

Continuing along the Via Flaminia, we come to the **Ponte Milvio**, the Milvian Bridge (also known as the Ponte Molle), which dates to the 1st century B.C.

In the area between Monte Mario and the Tiber is the **Foro Italico**.

The Church of Santa Maria sopra Minerva

From the Piazza Venezia, by way of the Via del Plebiscito, we reach the Piazza del Gesù, from where we turn right into the Via del Gesù and so arrive in the Piazza Minerva.

At the centre of the piazza is a small **Egyptian obelisk** (6th century B.C.) supported on the back of Bernini's marble **Elephant**. To the right is the **church of Santa Maria sopra Minerva**. Erected in the 8th century over the ruins of a temple dedicated to Minerva, the church has undergone various alterations and restorations. Its spacious interior is notable for its fine chapels containing some valuable works of art. We may mention, among the many: the Chapel of the Annunziata in the right aisle, designed by Carlo Maderno with a fine altarpiece by Antoniazzo Romano depicting «The Annunciation»; the Carafa Chapel in the right transept with wonderful frescoes by Filippino Lippi (1488-92) and tombs by Giuliano da Maiano and Giacomo Cosma (tomb of Guglielmo Durand by Giacomo Cosma); the Adobrandini Chapel in the right aisle by Giacomo Della Porta and Carlo Maderno with the monuments to the parents of Clement VIII by Nicolò Cordier; in the sanctuary, Michelangelo's statue of the «Redeemer»; in the chancel behind the high altar, the funerary monuments of Clement VII and Leo X designed by Antonio da Sangallo; the tomb of Cardinal Diego de Coca by Andrea Bregno.

Egyptian obelisk

Church Santa Maria sopra Minerva - Interior

The Pantheon

The Pantheon is one of the most important and most imposing of Roman temples: it is also the best preserved. It was built by Marcus Agrippa, son-in-law of Augustus, in 27 B.C., in honour of all the gods: hence its name.

Destroyed by a fire in 80 A.D., it was rebuilt in the time of Hadrian (between 110 and 125 A.D.). In 609 the temple was consecrated as a Christian church by Pope Boniface IV, who dedicated it to the Virgin Mary and all the Martyr Saints. The church became the burial place of illustrious Italian artists, such as Raphael Sanzio, the architects Baldassarre Peruzzi and Vignola, the painter Annibale Caracci, and also members of Italy's royal family: the Kings of Italy Victor Emanuel II and Umberto I and Queen Margherita.

The Pantheon is circular in plan, preceded by a pronaos of Greek type supported by sixteen monolithic granite columns surmounted by Corinthian capitals.

We enter the temple through an imposing bronze portal of Roman date.

The interior is majestic and highly original in its architecture. Rectangular alternating with semicircular niches are laid out round its walls. The hemispherical dome, of exceptional diameter (43.30 metres: equal to its maximum height from the floor), is decorated with coffering and illuminated by a central aperture some 9 metres in diameter.

Plastic model of the ancient Rome - The Pantheon

The Pantheon

The Pantheon - Interior

With regard to the building's sophisticated constructional technique, it seems that the skeleton of the dome consists of a series of ribs whose weight is supported on and relieved by the massive arches situated in the parts of the cylindrical walls not opened by the large niches. This and other ingenious architectural solutions make the Pantheon a wonderful monumental work in which grandeur of mass and gracefulness of line combine to form an awe-inspiring cohesion of effect.

The **church of San Luigi dei Francesi**, reachable by the Via Giustiniani, was erected in the 16th century by Domenico Fontana. Its interior houses important works by Caravaggio. In the street running parallel to it, the Corso del Rinascimento, is the **Palazzo Madama**, the seat of the Italian Senate since 1870. Decorated with a beautiful baroque façade, it contains a richly-endowed library of over 230,000 volumes. The building adjacent to it on the same street is occupied by the State Archives. It has a handsome courtyard, at the further end of which rises the **Chapel of Sant'Ivo della Sapienza**, by Borromini.

The Piazza Navona

From the Corso del Rinascimento we enter Piazza Navona. Situated on the site, and retaining the shape, of the ancient Stadium of Domitian, it represents one of the most popular and most characteristic centres of the city. The piazza is adorned with three fountains, of which the central one is the famous **Fountain of the Rivers**. Commissioned by Pope Innocent X as a setting for the obelisk that rises at its centre, it was sculpted by Bernini and some of his pupils in 1650-51. The four statues placed round the grotto at the foot of the obelisk represent four rivers: the Ganges, symbolising Asia, the Nile (Africa), the Danube (Europe) and the Plate (America). At the southern end of the Piazza Navona is the **Fountain of the Moor**, originally designed by Della Porta, but later modified by Bernini and Giovanni Mari.

At the other end of the piazza is the **Fountain of Neptune**. Originally designed by Della Porta and partially realized by Bernini, this fountain long remained incomplete. It was not completed till 1878 when the sculptor Antonio Della Bitta added the statue of Neptune from which it takes its name.

Facing onto the Fountain of the Rivers is the **church of Sant'Agnese in Agone** (17th century), a masterpiece of baroque architecture by Rainaldi and Borromini, who designed its façade and dome.

The piazza is completed by a further three buildings: the **church of San Giacomo degli Spagnoli**, the **Palazzo Lancellotti**, and the **Palazzo Pamphilj**. The latter, built by Rainaldi for Innocent X in 1650, is now the Brazilian Embassy, and contains a large hall with frescoes by Pietro da Cortona.

Adjacent to the piazza are two other churches: the **church of Santa Maria dell'Anima** (16th century) and the **church of Santa Maria della Pace** (15th century).

From here we reach the Piazza di Tor Sanguigna, and make our way along the Via del Governo Vecchio, on which is situated the **Palazzo del Governo Vecchio**, erected in the 15th century. Further on is the **Palazzo del Banco di Santo Spirito**, the former papal mint designed by Antonio da Sangallo the Younger, while nearby is the **church of San Salvatore in Lauro**, situated in the piazza of the same name.

The Piazza Navona

Aerial view of the Piazza Navona

Returning in the direction of Piazza Navona by way of the Via dei Coronari, we can visit the **church of Sant'Apollinare** and the **church of Sant'Agostino**. The latter, built in the 15th century by Giacomo da Pietrasanta using blocks of travertine spoliated from the Colosseum, has an elegant façade in the Renaissance style and is topped by the first dome to be built in the city since Roman times. Some notable works of art are preserved in its interior, such as Sansovino's statue of the «Madonna del Parto»; Raphael's fresco of «Isaiah»; Caravaggio's altarpiece of the «Madonna of the Pilgrims»; and Guercino's «Saints Augustine, John and Jerome». Worth visiting nearby is the **Palazzo Primoli** (Via Zanardelli) which now

houses the **Napoleonic Museum** containing a rich collection of objects belonging to the Bonaparte family. On the Via dei Portoghesi not far away is the **church of Sant'Antonio dei Portoghesi**, built in the early years of the 15th century but remodelled in the baroque style by Martino Longhi in the 17th. It contains Vanvitelli's beautiful **Altar of the Concession**.
In a side-street (Via San Clementino) of the Via della Scrofa stands the huge **Palazzo Borghese**, built for Cardinal Dezza in 1590 and subsequently transformed by Flaminio Ponzio. The palace is entered through a large and majestic portal, which leads into the magnificent courtyard, with a garden ornamented with antiquities and fountains at its further end. We now reach

the Via di Ripetta on which are situated the **churches of San Girolamo degli Illirici** (16th century) and **San Rocco**, erected in 1499 and with a handsome façade by Valadier. Adjacent to the latter is the **Mausoleum of Augustus**, built by Augustus himself in 28 B.C. as a tomb for his family. Following centuries of abandonment, it was finally restored to its original appearance in 1936. Opposite it is one of the most important Roman monuments in the city: the **Ara Pacis Augustae**, erected between 13 and 9 B.C. to celebrate the peace established by Augustus throughout the Roman world. Further on, on the Via di Ripetta, is the **Institute of Fine Arts**, Rome's main art school built by Camprese in the 19th century.

We now visit the **church of the Gesù**, which we can reach from the Piazza Venezia by taking the Via del Plebiscito until we come to the Piazza del Gesù on which the church stands. Begun by Vignola in the mid-16th century, it presents a wide and handsome façade by Giacomo Della Porta. The Gesù, mother church of the Jesuits, has a beautiful interior sumptuously decorated with frescoes, stuccoes, bronzes and polychrome marbles; again, the basic design is by Vignola. Particularly important and very spectacular is the fresco of the vault over the nave, representing the Triumph of the Name of Jesus, by Baciccia (Giovan Battista Gaulli), who was also responsible for the frescoes in the dome and chancel. In the left transept is the Chapel of St. Ignatius of Loyola, the richly decorated monument to the founder of the Jesuits, a late-17th century work by Andrea Pozzo.

From the Gesù we continue along the **Corso Vittorio Emanuele II**, the wide thoroughfare swept through the city in 1881, and so arrive in the **Largo Argentina**, the large square in which have been excavated the remains of the **Area Sacra**, at one time the centre of the Campus Martius. The archaeological excavations which explored the site in the early years of the century revealed one of the most interesting monumental complexes of Republican Rome, consisting of four temples, of which one circular; their identification is uncertain.

Further ahead, on the Corso Vittorio, is the **Piazza di Sant'Andrea della Valle**, dominated by the church of the same name. Begun in the late 16th century by Grimaldi and Giacomo Della Porta, it was later completed by Carlo Maderno, who also designed the large 17th century dome. In the mid-17th century Carlo Rainaldi made alterations to the building, and gave it a sumptuous and imposing appearance especially by the addition of the façade. The church contains the tombs of the Piccolomini Popes (Pius II and Pius III), transferred here from St. Peter's, and also magnificent frescoes by Domenichino. Continuing along the Corso Vittorio, we see to the right the **Palazzo Massimo alle Colonne**, built by Peruzzi in c. 1530; the building presents a curving rusticated façade pierced by elegant windows. Its courtyard, embellished with ancient statues and other antiquities, is of some interest. Just after it is the **church of San Pantaleo** on the piazza of the same name, erected in 1216 but reconstructed at a later period. To one side of the piazza stands the **Palazzo Braschi**, the seat of the **Museum of Rome** since 1952; it contains interesting collections of art relating to the history of the city from medieval to modern times. The third floor of the building houses the **Contemporary Gallery of Modern Art**, in which a rich collection of works by Roman artists of the 19th century is displayed. Crossing over to the other side of the Corso Vittorio we see the **Palazzetto**

della Piccola Farnesina, an elegant 16th century town house which now houses the **Barracco Museum** (ancient sculptures), the donation of Baron G. Barracco. It is followed by the **Palazzo della Cancelleria**, built in the Renaissance style, according to some, by Bramante, who was probably the architect of the magnificent courtyard. Adjacent is the **church of San Lorenzo in Damaso**; a church with very ancient origins, it was restored by Valadier in the early 19th century. From the piazza in front of the church we can enter the **Campo de' Fiori**, a piazza notorious for the sentences of death that were carried out in it and that drew crowds of spectators. Today it is the site of a lively and picturesque fruit and vegetable market. At the centre of the piazza stands the **bronze monument to Giordano Bruno**, the well-known philosopher who was burnt here as a heretic in 1600. Turning into the Via della Corda, we now reach the harmonious **Piazza Farnese**, decorated by two twin fountains by Rainaldi (the huge granite tubs come from the Baths of Caracalla) and dominated by the 16th century **Palazzo Farnese**. Begun by Antonio Sangallo, it was continued by Michelangelo and completed by Giacomo Della Porta. Its majestic façade topped by a magnificent cornice decorated with the Farnese lilies is by Michelangelo. The palace is entered through Antonio Sangallo's barrel-vaulted atrium, which leads into the courtyard containing two sarcophagi from the Baths of Caracalla and the Tomb of Cecilia Metella. On the first floor is the **Gallery** frescoed by Annibale Carracci assisted by his brother and by Domenichino. The sumptuous Salon, occupying two floors of the palace in height, is decorated with a handsome coffered ceiling and tapestry reproduction of Raphael frescoes; also of interest are Guglielmo Della Porta's two sculptures of « Peace » and « Abundance ». Another room in the palace (the **Sala dei Fasti Farnesiani**) has magnificent frescoes by Salviati and Zuccari celebrating the exploits of the Farnese family.

Nearby is the **Palazzo Spada**, erected by Giulio Merisi da Caravaggio in 1540, but later transformed by Borromini. It houses the **Galleria Spada** containing distinguished works of art of the 16th and 17th century, including: « Portrait of Cardinal Spada » by **Guido Reni**; « Portrait of a Musician » by **Titian**; and « Portrait of a Cardinal » by **Rubens.**

We now make our way back to the Corso Vittorio Emanuele, and come to the large **church of Santa Maria in Vallicella**, better known as the **Chiesa Nuova**. Begun in 1575, it was built over the preexisting church of San Giovanni (12th century), and designed by the architect Martino Longhi the Elder. The central portal is surmounted by a sumptuous loggia and some statues. The interior contains, among others, works by Barocci, Algardi and Rubens. Next to it stands the **Oratory of St. Philip Neri**, erected by Borromini in 1640. At the end of the Corso Vittorio, the Lungotevere dei Fiorentini leads to the bridge over the Tiber: the Ponte Principe Amedeo di Savoia Aosta, close to which rises the elegantly elliptical dome (designed by Maderno) of the **church of San Giovanni dei Fiorentini** (16th century). It looks onto the Via Giulia, which is notable for the many Renaissance palaces by which it is flanked, including the 16th century **Palazzo Donarelli** and **Palazzo Sacchetti**. In a little side street a little further along is the small **church of Sant'Eligio degli Orefici** (on the Via Sant'Eligio), built in 1516 and designed by Raphael.

Trastevere

Again departing from Piazza Venezia, we take the Corso Vittorio Emanuele to the Largo Argentina, and from here turn left into the Via Arenula which leads to the Ponte Garibaldi over the Tiber. On the other side of the bridge we enter on the characteristic district of **Trastevere**. This picturesque quarter of Rome still keeps alive its own popular traditions, and even its own dialect, which help to give it a lively and colourful atmosphere and make it the stimulating centre of local bohemian life.

From the bridge we enter the **Piazza Gioacchino Belli** with its statue of the famous poet of the same name, the author of many sonnets in the Roman dialect. It is followed by the Piazza Sonnino with the **Torre degli Anguillara**, one of the few surviving medieval towers (13th century). At the beginning of the Viale Trastevere is the **church of San Crisogono**, dating back to the 5th century but successively remodelled; the Romanesque belltower and the apse are in fact later (12th century). The façade is preceded by a 17th century portico, and the interior contains frescoes by Guercino and a mosaic attributed to pupils of Cavallini.

We now turn into the Via dei Genovesi on which the **church of San Giovanni dei Genovesi** is situated; founded in the 15th century, it was reconstructed in 1864. To its left is the **Hospice of the Genovesi** with a 15th century cloister considered one of the finest of the period.

In the nearby **Piazza di Santa Cecilia** stands the **church** of the same name, of ancient origins, but radically altered in the 18th century, including the addition of its late-baroque façade by Ferdinando Fuga; it is flanked by a Romanesque bell-tower. The interior contains a monument by Mino da Fiesole, a 13th century ciborium by Arnolfo di Cambio, and a fine statue of Saint Cecilia by Maderno. In the convent annexed to the church is a valuable fresco by Pietro Cavallini depicting « The Last Judgement ».

From the Via Anicia we reach the Piazza di San Francesco d'Assisi, whence we continue by the Via San Francesco a Ripa to the **Basilica of Santa Maria in Trastevere**. The church, among the first to be consecrated in Rome, was begun in the 3rd century and completed in 341-52. Reconstructed in the 12th century, it has over the centuries undergone a series of alterations but these have not involved substantial changes to its basic appearance. The Romanesque bell-tower and mosaic-decorated façade date to the 12th century; the portico in front was added in the 18th (Carlo Fontana). The magnificent interior, divided into a nave and two aisles by ancient columns, has splendid mosaics by Pietro Cavallini in the apse.

Just beyond the nearby Piazza Sant'Egidio is the **church of Santa Maria della Scala** (late 16th century), based on a design by Francesco da Volterra; worth noting inside is Rainaldi's baldacchino over the high altar. In the Via Corsini is the large Palazzo Corsini, dating to the 15th century, but completely transformed by Ferdinando Fuga in 1732-36. It houses the **National Gallery of Ancient Art**, comprising a fine collection of works by Italian and foreign artists of the 17th and 18th century, including: « St. Sebastian » by Rubens; « Rest on the Flight into Egypt » by Van Dyck; « St. John the Baptist » by Caravaggio; and « Views of Venice » by Canaletto. The palace is also the seat of Italy's most ancient academy, founded by Federico Cesi in the early 17th century: the **Accademia Nazionale dei Lincei**. Facing the Palazzo Corsini is the beautiful early 16th century **Villa Farnesina**, designed by Baldassare Peruzzi. Its interior was decorated by the leading artists of the day, including Raphael, who painted the famous « Story of Psyche » (on the ceiling of the gallery) and the fresco of « Galatea » which adorns another of the ground-floor rooms. On the first floor are paintings by Sodoma (« Nuptials of Alexander and Roxana »), Peruzzi and others. The building also houses the **Gabinetto Nazionale delle Stampe**: an important collection of prints and drawings (from the 15th century on).

Continuing along the Via della Lungara, we come to the late 16th century **Palazzo Salviati**. Behind it, on the slopes of the Janiculum, is the 15th century **church of Sant'Onofrio**, with frescoes by Domenichino in the portico. Inside, in the apse, are frescoes by Peruzzi. The church contains a monument to Torquato Tasso, the 16th century poet who died in the adjoining convent where a little museum devoted to him has been installed. At the end of Via della Lungara is the **Porta di Santo Spirito**, a gateway designed by Sangallo. To our left rise the slopes of the Janiculum, a delightful hill of trees and gardens and panoramic views over the city. It is also associated with historical memories of the Risorgimento, commemorated by the monument to Giuseppe Garibaldi (by Gallori). Also on the hill is the **Villa Doria Pamphilj**; at the centre of its huge park stands the charming Casino designed by Algardi.

Very close to the entrance to the Villa Doria Pamphilj are the **church of San Pancrazio**, built over the site of the catacombs of the same name (which may be visited by descending from the church), and the **Fountain of the Acqua Paola**, built for Pope Paul V by Flaminio Ponzio. Worth visiting near the latter is the **church of San Pietro in Montorio**, situated in the little piazza of the same name commanding fine panoramic views over Rome. Erected, according to tradition, on the site where St. Peter was crucified, the church has been successively restored in the course of the centuries. Its interior contains some notable works of art, including Pomarancio's « Madonna of the Letter » and the Raimondi Chapel designed by Bernini. In a courtyard adjacent to the church is Bramante's **Tempietto**, a circular chapel in the classical style built by the artist for Ferdinand of Spain between 1499 and 1502. Restored at a later date, it contains some sculptures of the school of Bernini. From here we may visit the **Villa Sciarra** (reachable by way of the Via Garibaldi and then the Via Fabrizi), a 15th century building once the property of the noble family after whom it is named and later the residence of an American diplomat, who left it to the city. It is surrounded by an attractive public park adorned with charming fountains. Not far away, just off the Via Garibaldi, is another garden, the **Bosco Parrasio**, once the pastoral rendez-vous of a group of 18th century literati.

Basilica of Santa Maria in Trastevere

The Fountain of the Acqua Paola   **The Tempietto di San Pietro in Montorio**

The Castel Sant'Angelo

Intended by the emperor Hadrian as the burial place for himself and members of his family, it was erected on the site of the ancient Horti Domizia. The bridge in front of it, the present Ponte Sant'Angelo, the ancient **Pons Aelius**, linked the mausoleum with the centre of Rome. Later turned into a fortress, the **Mausoleum of Hadrian** assumed the name of **Castel Sant'Angelo**, and became a prison in which such famous characters as Giordano Bruno and Cagliostro were incarcerated. It now houses a **museum** which contains various exhibits relating to its construction and history, including the strongboxes that used to contain the church treasures salvaged by the Popes, who used the Castel Sant'Angelo as a fortress and refuge in times of peril. We may also visit the beautifully decorated and frescoed papal apartments and the cells of the prisoners.

Castel Sant'Angelo

Plastic model of the ancient Rome - Castel Sant'Angelo

Bridge and Castel Sant'Angelo

St. Peter Basilica ➤

Vatican City

The Vatican City is an independent state whose sovereign head is the Pope, Bishop of Rome and Supreme Pontiff of the Catholic Church.

The Vatican state, which was created following the Lateran Treaty on 11 February 1929, occupies the Ager Vaticanus, on the right bank of the Tiber, the site on which the first Christians, including St. Peter himself, were martyred.

St. Peter's Basilica — In the year 324 Constantine, himself a convert to Christianity, erected a sumptuous basilica in honour of the Apostle. Enriched and embellished throughtout the Middle Ages, this early Christian basilica eventually became so delapidated that it was decided to rebuild it completely: the commission to do was entrusted to Bramante in 1506. In the years that followed numerous alterations to the original plans were made, and Raphael, Peruzzi, Sangallo and Michelangelo were all successively involved in the project as architects. The latter, basing himself in part on Bramante's plan (which had already begun to be built) conceived a huge basilica on a Greek-cross plan, topped by a magnificent double-shell dome. In the early years of the 17th century Maderno transformed the Greek-cross into a Latin-cross plan by elongating the nave, and also designed the existing façade. Later Bernini laid out the elliptical colonnade embracing St. Peter's Square.

St. Peter's Square is reached by the Via della Conciliazione. At its centre stands an Egyptian obelisk which originally graced the Circus of Nero and was raised here in 1586. It is flanked by two fountains respectively built by Maderno and Bernini. The façade of the basilica behind is approached by a stairway on three levels.

St. Peter's Basilica

The façade with a broad central portico presents a series of nine balconies, of which the central one is called the **Loggia of the Benedictions**. It is in fact from this balcony that the Pontiff imparts the « Urbi et Orbi » blessing to the numerous faithful who throng St. Peter's Square. Five entrances, flanked by gigantic marble Corinthian columns which rise to the top of the façade, lead into the **Atrium**, magnificently designed by Maderno and decorated with splendid stuccoes and mosaics. Above the central doorway is Giotto's famous mosaic of the **Navicella** (the allegorical ship carrying the disciples), while to the right of the portico, behind a glass door, is Bernini's **equestrian statue of the emperor Constantine**.

The central bronze door leading into the basilica was the work of the sculptor Antonio Filarete (1440-1445); a masterpiece of bronzesmith's work, its reliefs include scenes of the martyrdoms of Saints Peter and Paul. The last door to the right is the **Porta Santa**, the door famous throughout the world which the Pope opens at the beginning of Jubilee years, symbolically using a ceremonial hammer.

St. Peter Basilica and "Via della Conciliazione"

We now enter the Basilica. We immediately realize that we have entered the largest and most grandiose sacred building extant: a building vast in scale and awe-inspiring in effect, conceived to celebrate the sacrality of the Catholic Church and as such full of sacred relics and wonderful works of art in a splendid fusion of the Renaissance and Baroque.

In the **central nave**, at the beginning of which are two holy water stoups supported by putti (18th century), is the venerated **bronze statue of St. Peter** (13th century). A series of chapels open up along the aisles. They include (on the right) the **Chapel of the Pietà**, with its famous Michelangelo statue of the dead body of Christ lying in the lap of his Mother: the «**Pietà**», which the artist sculpted at the age of 24. This is followed in the **right aisle** by: the **Chapel of St. Sebastian**, with a mosaic representing the martyrdom of the Saint by Domenichino; the **Chapel of the Holy Sacrament**, with its magnificently decorated gilt bronze ciborium by Bernini; and the **Gregorian Chapel**, ornately decorated by Giacomo Della Porta, with a 12th century icon of the Virgin Mary (the «Madonna del Soccorso») on its altar.

In the **right transept**, in the passage to the Chapel of St. Michael, is Canova's monument to Clement XIII Rezzonico, while in the **Chapel of St. Michael** is a mosaic copy of Guido Reni's painting of the Saint.

In the **apse** is the **Cathedra Petri**, a sumptuous baroque complex of gilt bronze created by Bernini as a setting to enclose the ancient wooden throne used, according to tradition, by Saint Peter; it is supported by monumental figures of the four Fathers of the Church. To the side of the apse are two papal tombs: Bernini's monument to the Barberini Pope Urban VIII, and Giacomo Della Porta's monument to Paul III.

Let us now look upwards and admire Michelangelo's gigantic **dome**, considered the largest masonry construction of its kind. The dome, some 120 m. high, is supported by four mighty piers, in the faces of which Bernini hewed out four niches containing the colossal statues of St. Helena, St. Veronica, St. Longinus and St. Andrew. At the centre-point below the dome is Bernini's **Baldacchino**, the magnificent bronze canopy over the shrine of the Apostle made, according to the legend, from the bronze stripped from the pronaos of the Pantheon.

To the left of the apse is the **Chapel of the Column**: it contains Algardi's marble altarpiece of «The Meeting between Leo the Great and Attila» and the tomb of the Pope. Before entering the left transept we pass the tomb of Pope Alexander VII, sculpted by Bernini and some of his pupils.

In the **left transept** are three altars decorated with wonderful mosaic copies of paintings, representing: «St. Joseph», «Doubting Thomas» and the «Crucifixion of St. Peter».

In the passage we see, over the entrance to the sacristy, the monument to Pius VIII, and then enter the **Clementine Chapel**, completed by Giacomo Della Porta and containing the tomb of Pius VII by Thorvaldsen.

We now enter the **left aisle**: in the passage to the right is the monument of Leo XI by Algardi. It is followed by the **Chapel of the Choir**, decorated with beautiful 16th century stuccoes. Just past it, to the left, is the bronze tomb of Pope Innocent

St. Peter Basilica - Interior

La Pietà of Michelangelo

St. Peter's Chair (Bernini)

Interior of St. Peter's Dome

VIII by Pollaiolo (transferred here from the old basilica). Next is the **Chapel of the Presentation** and, in the passage to the Baptistery, the monument to the last Stuarts by Canova. At the foot of the left aisle is the **Baptistery**: the Font consists of the cover of an ancient porphyry sarcophagus.

We can now visit the Sacristy, erected by Marchionni in 1776-84. It provides access to the **Treasury of St. Peter**, consisting of precious liturgical objects and donations made by the faithful over the centuries. Among the most striking exhibits are a 4th century sarcophagus, the magnificent **Crux Vaticana** richly studded with precious gems (6th century) and Pollaiolo's bronze monument of the Della Rovere Pope Sixtus IV (15th century). Below the Basilica are the Vatican Crypts **(Grotte Vaticane)** which contain a collection of Early Christian sarcophagi and numerous tombs of Popes. The entrance to the Crypts is under the crossing.

The Vatican Palaces

The fascinating group of buildings we are about to describe has claims to be considered the most important architectural complex extant, both from the artistic and historical viewpoint. The **Vatican Palaces**, the official entrance to which is through the **Bronze Portal** to the right of St. Peter's, have undergone numerous alterations, enlargements and embellishments in the course of the centuries, and some of the most famous artists of all time have contributed to them, including Michelangelo, Bramante, Raphael and Bernini. The latter designed the majestic **Scala Regia**, the grand ceremonial staircase which leads up to the **Sala Regia** (audience hall) and the **Pauline Chapel**, decorated with beautiful frescoes by Michelangelo. The **Pontifical Apostolic Palace** is only visitable on the occasion of audiences with the Pope, who currently resides in the building added to the complex by Sixtus V. His official apartment, in which he carries out his main engagements, is on its second floor, and is preceded by the richly decorated **Clementine Hall**, to which access is given by the Papal Stairway.

The Vatican Museums

Entered from the Viale del Vaticano, the various sectors of the Museum are reached by ascending the impressive **Spiral Staircase**. From here the Museums of Antiquities are situated to our left, the Picture Gallery (Pinacoteca) straight ahead, and the Museo Gregoriano Profano and Museo Pio Cristiano to our right.

The Vatican Picture Gallery

Arranged in its present building by Pius XI, the Vatican Picture Gallery (the **Pinacoteca Vaticana**) consists of 15 rooms in which important paintings stretching from the primitives to the 18th century are displayed:
Room 1. The Primitives: «The Last Judgement», a work of the 11th century by the masters Giovanni and Niccolò;
Room 2. School of Giotto and Late Gothic Masters: the room is dominated by the «Stefaneschi Triptych», by pupils of Giotto;

Cappella Paolina - Interior

Cappella Paolina - St. Peter's Crucifixion ➤

Room 3. Fra Angelico, Filippo Lippi and Benozzo Gozzoli: Fra Angelico is represented by «Episodes from the Life of St. Nicholas» and the «Madonna and Child between Saints»;

Room 4. Melozzo da Forlì: «Sixtus IV appointing Platina Prefect of the Vatican Library» and «Music-making Angels», fragments of a lost fresco by Melozzo;

Room 5. Lesser Masters of the 15th century: «The Miracles of St. Vincent Ferrer» and «Pietà» (Lucas Cranach);

Room 6. Polyptychs: especially noteworthy is a work by Crivelli: «Madonna and Child» (1482);

Room 7. Umbrian paintings of the 15th century: they include works by Perugino and Pinturicchio;

Room 8. Raphael: «Coronation of the Virgin» which the artist painted at the age of twenty; it undoubtedly represents one of the most significant works of this great painter, who was a pupil of Perugino;

Room 9. Leonardo da Vinci: «St. Jerome», an unfinished work;

Room 10. Titian: «Madonna of St. Niccolò dei Frari».

This is followed by **Room 11**, with works by 16th century artists; **Room 12** or Baroque Room, dedicated to the painters of the 17th century with the famous «Deposition» by Caravaggio; **Rooms 13 and 14**, in which works of the 17th and 18th century are displayed; and lastly **Room 15** or Room of the Portraits.

On leaving the Picture Gallery we come (on the left) to the **Museo Gregoriano Profano**: transferred from the Lateran to the Vatican by John XXIII in recent times, it comprises Roman sculptures from the 1st to the 3rd century A.D.

Museo Pio Cristiano: founded by Pius IX in the 19th century, it comprises numerous Christian artefacts found in the Catacombs and in ancient churches.

Ethnological Missionary Museum: inaugurated in 1927, it comprises material relating to non-European cultures donated to the Museum both by numerous bequests made by the Missions and by the Missionary Exhibition (1925).

THE MUSEUMS OF ANTIQUITIES

They contain as a whole the richest collection of classical art in the world. The collection is due to the interest taken by various Popes, such as Clement XIV, Pius VI, Pius VII and Gregory XVI who reorganized and enlarged the collection of Roman antiquities already amassed during the Renaissance.

GREGORIAN EGYPTIAN MUSEUM - Founded by Gregory XVI, it contains sarcophagi, mummies, grave goods and other artefacts relating to the civilization of ancient Egypt.

PIO-CLEMENTINE MUSEUM - The magnificent Roman statues displayed in this museum include the marble «Apollo Belvedere», a copy of a 4th century B.C. original; the famous marble group of «Laocoon» dating to the 1st century B.C.-1st century A.D.; and the «Hermes», a copy of the original by Praxiteles.

CHIARAMONTI MUSEUM - In the long gallery in which it is housed are displayed a large number of ancient sculptures. The Museum has two further sections: the **Galleria Lapidaria** and the **Braccio Nuovo**, comprising a striking Roman statue of a river-god representing the Nile.

We now return to the Vestibule of the Museums of Sculpture to visit the Hall of the Chariot (**Sala della Biga**), so-called be-

Vatican Picture Gallery - The Virgin Mary with St. Dominic and St. Catherine (Beato Angelico)

Vatican Picture Gallery - The Transfiguration - Detail ➤ (Raphael)

cause of the presence at its centre of a Roman chariot of the 1st century B.C. The room also contains the «Discobolos» by Myron, a statue of Dionysus and some sarcophagi of children. To our right is the long **Gallery of the Candelabra**, consisting of six sections in which are displayed a variety of ancient sculptures, copies of ancient candelabra, sarcophagi and fragments of precious frescoes.

GREGORIAN ETRUSCAN MUSEUM - It too founded by Pope Gregory XVI, it consists of nine rooms in which are displayed interesting archaeological material recovered from the main Etruscan cemetery sites: sarcophagi, cinerary urns, terracottas and valuable collections of Etruscan gold jewellery. We return to the Gallery of the Candelabra, through which we reach the **Gallery of the Tapestries** in which are hung ten wonderful tapestries based on cartoons by pupils of Raphael. It is followed by the **Gallery of the Geographical Maps**, a corridor over 100 metres long whose walls are adorned with painted maps of Italy and her regions.

It leads, in turn into the **Gallery of St. Pius V**, consisting of two rooms containing specimens of medieval fabrics and the gallery proper in which some beautiful tapestries are displayed.

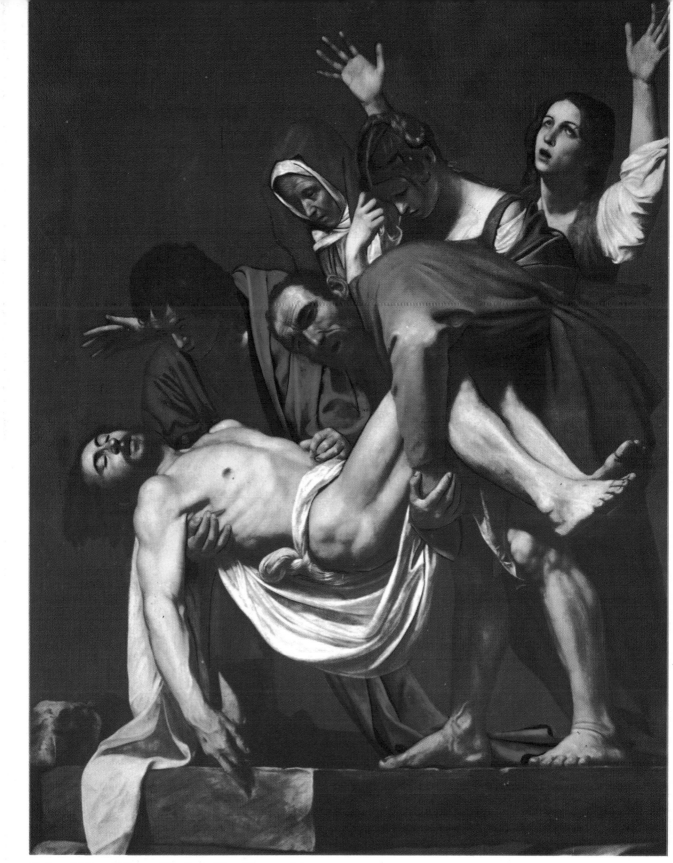

Vatican Picture Gallery - The Deposition (Caravaggio)

Chiaramonti Museum - The New Wing   **Chiaramonti Museum - The New Wing - The Nile**

The Belvedere Courtyard - The Laocoon Group

The Sistine Chapel

Designed by the architect Giovannino de' Dolci for Pope Sixtus IV, it represents one of the most important complexes both from an artistic and a religious and historical point of view. It consists of a large rectangular hall, surmounted by a richly frescoed barrel vault. The **Sistine Chapel** is still the venue of important church ceremonies, notably the **Conclave**. This traditional meeting of the Cardinals is aimed at electing the new Pope and communicating the outcome to the faithful by means of a smoke signal, black smoke indicating the inconclusiveness of the vote and the continuation of the meeting, white smoke announcing the new nomination.

The frescoes of the walls of the Sistine Chapel date to 1481-83; those of the ceiling to a quarter century later. The painters involved in this sublime work of pictorial decoration include the most authoritative names in the whole world of Italian painting: first and foremost **Michelangelo**, then **Pinturicchio** and **Signorelli** and the most noted representatives of the Florentine school, such as **Botticelli, Ghirlandaio** and **Cosimo Rosselli**. Let us now take a closer look at the frescoes, starting from the altar and continuing along the wall to the left:

1st painting: «The circumcision of Moses» and «The sojourn of Moses in Egypt», by **Pinturicchio** and **Perugino**.

2nd painting: «Moses driving away the Midianites from the well, the killing of the Egyptian and the daughters of Jethro», by **Botticelli**.

3rd painting: «Passage of the Red Sea», by **Cosimo Rosselli**.

4th painting: «Moses receiving the tables of the Law on Mount Sinai and the adoration of the Golden Calf», by **Cosimo Rosselli**.

5th painting: «Punishment of Korah, Dathan and Abiram», an illustrious example of the art of **Botticelli**.

6th painting: «The reading of Moses' testament and the handing over of the rod, symbol of authority, to his successor», a masterpiece of the art of **Luca Signorelli**.

The other series of frescoes on the opposite wall depicts some episodes from the earthly life of Jesus. Again starting out from the altar, we see:

1st painting: «The baptism of Christ», by **Pinturicchio and Perugino**.

2nd painting: «The temptations of Jesus and the purification of the leper», by **Botticelli**.

3rd painting: «The calling of Saints Peter and Andrew», by **Ghirlandaio**.

4th painting: «The sermon on the mount and the healing of the leper», by **Cosimo Rosselli**.

5th painting: «The handing over of the keys to St. Peter», a masterpiece by **Perugino**.

6th painting: «The Last Supper», by **Cosimo Rosselli**.

The frescoing of the ceiling vault was commissioned by Pope Julius II from Michelangelo, who completed the work in the space of three years (1508-1512). This work of incomparable grandeur, though consisting of various scenes, is incredibly unified and homogeneous in effect. All round the lower part of the ceiling the master depicted 12 huge and majestic figures of **Prophets** and **Sibyls**, seated on marble thrones. The Sibyls are alternated with the figures of Prophets, since they too had, in the pagan world, predicted the coming of a different era characterized by another way of understanding man and life proper to Christianity. The central part of the ceiling, divided into panels by architectural frames and interspersed with the nude figures known as **Ignudi**, represents scenes from Genesis. Starting from the gigantic figure of the Prophet Jonah above the altar, we see:

— «The Creation of Light»
— «The Creation of the Stars and of Plants»
— «God the Father circling in the infinite, separating the land from the water»
— «The Creation of Adam»
— «The Creation of Eve»
— «The Fall and Expulsion from Paradise»
— «The Sacrifice of Noah»
— «The Flood»
— «The Drunkenness of Noah»

Two spandrels of the vault to the side of the Prophet Jonah are frescoed with «The Brazen Serpent» and «The Punishment of Haman», while the corresponding spandrels on the opposite side of the ceiling, separated by the Prophet Zachariah, represent «Judith and Holofernes» and «David and Goliath».

The end wall of the Chapel, between the two series of lateral frescoes, is the wonderful wall behind the altar painted by Michelangelo with «The Last Judgement». Begun in July 1536, it was painted by the master after the decoration of the rest of the chapel had been completed. The scene describes with dramatic crescendo and great sense of movement the turmoil, the agitation, the mood of heightened expectation of all the figures surrounding Christ, at the centre, severe and implacable in his role as Judge. Below to the right we see the figures of the sinners massed together in the boat guided by Charon who is leading them to the underworld. Above him, cloud-borne angels sound the trumpets of judgement. At the feet of Christ are Saints Laurence and Bartholomew, the latter bearing the emblems of his martyrdom, the knife and flayed skin, whose face is that of the artist himself. Particularly delicate is the figure of the Virgin Mary at Christ's side.

The pictures of the Sixtine Chapel's vaults show the ➤ Frescoes as they can be admired today, after a new restoration.

The photograph related to the back walls of the same chapel represents "The Last Judgement".

It was obtained by means of a computer device, that is to say, it was "cleaned" in order to produce a faithful copy of the colours originally used for it, and presently brought to light by the latest restoration.

THE CEILING
OF THE
SISTINE CHAPEL

THE PROPHET JEREMIAH

THE PERSIAN SIBYL

THE PROPHET EZECHIEL

THE ERYTHRAEAN SIBYL

THE PROPHET JOEL

THE PROPHET JONAH

THE CREATION OF
LIGHT

THE CREATION OF THE
STARS AND OF PLANTS

GOD THE FATHER
CIRCLING IN THE
INFINITE, SEPARATING
THE LAND FROM THE
WATER

THE CREATION OF
ADAM

THE CREATION OF EVE

THE FALL AND
EXPULSION FROM
PARADISE

THE SACRIFICE OF NOAH

THE FLOOD

THE DRUNKENNES OF
NOAH

THE PROPHET
ZACHARIAH

THE LIBYAN SIBYL

THE PROPHET DANIEL

THE CUMAEAN SIBYL

THE PROPHET ISAIAH

THE DELPHIC SIBYL

ESAIAS

◄ **Vault of the Chapel - The Creation of the Man (Michelangelo)**   **The Flood** (Michelangelo)

The Stanze of Raphael

The suite of rooms known as the **Stanze** was frescoed by the artist on the commission of Pope Julius II, who wanted to transfer his residence from the Borgia Apartment to the second floor of the Papal Palace. The work was begun by **Raphael Sanzio**, then only 25 years old, in the autumn of 1508. The Pope was so struck by the genius and inspiration of the young artist that he gave him sole charge of the work, removing the commission he had previously entrusted to other distinguished artists, such as Signorelli, Pinturicchio, Perugino and Sodoma.

We now enter the first of the four rooms that make up the **Stanze**: this is the **Room of the « Fire in the Borgo »**. It is decorated with the famous fresco from which it takes its name, situated on the wall facing the window. It depicts the fire which broke out in the Borgo — the district adjacent to the Vatican — in the year 847, and which was miraculously quenched by Leo IV by the sign of the cross.

The second room is the so-called **Sala della Segnatura**: it was the first to be frescoed with themes relating to the four principles of human knowledge: Theology, represented by the « Disputation of the Sacrament » (or the **Disputa** as it is more commonly called); Philosophy with the « School of Athens »; Poetry with the « Parnassus »; and Justice with the figure of a woman, severe in aspect, accompanied by the inscription « Ius suum unicuique tribuit ».

The third of the rooms is the **Room of Heliodorus**: it derives its name from the large fresco situated on the wall facing the entrance and depicting « The Expulsion of Heliodorus from the Temple ». The room also contains frescoes of « Leo I stopping the Invasion of Attila », « The Miracle of Bolsena » and « The Liberation of St. Peter from Prison ».

The fourth room is the **Room of Constantine**: only completed after the death of Raphael by his pupils, it takes its name from the huge fresco of the « Battle of Constantine » which fills the long wall facing the window.

After visiting the **Stanze** of Raphael, we can pass into the adjoining **Logge**, a long gallery in 13 bays designed by Bramante and frescoed by pupils of Raphael, based on designs he himself had produced before his premature death. The scenes portrayed are taken from the Old and New Testament.

From the Room of Constantine we can also visit the **Chapel of Nicholas V**, magnificently decorated with frescoes by Fra Angelico with scenes taken from the lives of Saints Laurence and Stephen.

Raphael's Stanze - Room of the Fire in the Borgo

Raphael's Stanze - "The Disputation of the Sacrament"

Raphael's Stanze - The School of Athens

Raphael's Stanze - Parnassus

Raphael's Stanze - The Expulsion of Heliodorus from the Temple

Raphael's Stanze - The Miracle of Bolsena

Raphael's Stanze - The Liberation of St. Peter from Prison

Hall of Constantine - The Battle of Milvian Bridge

Hall of Constantine - The Baptism of Constantine

Loggias of Raphael ➤

The Borgia Apartment

This was the residence inside the Papal Palace of Pope Alexander VI (the Borgia Pope). He entrusted the decoration of the rooms of the apartment to the Sienese painter Pinturicchio, who completed the work together with some of his assistants in the period 1492-95. The Borgia Apartment consists of six rooms:

Room 1 is the **Room of the Sibyls**: it has 12 lunettes frescoed with Sibyls and Prophets.

Room 2 is the **Room of the Credo**: it derives its name from the 12 pairs of Prophets and Apostles in the lunettes, who are accompanied with verses from the Credo.

Room 3 is the **Room of the Liberal Arts**: this was in fact the room used by Alexander VI as a dining-room; it was frescoed by Antonio di Viterbo with representations of the «Liberal Arts».

Room 4 is the **Room of the Saints**: almost entirely decorated by Pinturicchio, the room is notable for its beautiful frescoes, of which we may note in particular the «Disputation of St. Catherine of Alexandria before the emperor Maximian».

Room 5 is the **Room of the Mysteries**: the lunettes that decorate the room, they too by Pinturicchio, are frescoed with episodes from the life of Christ.

Room 6 is the **Room of the Popes**: it is decorated with stuccoes and fantastic grottesche by Perin del Vaga and Giovanni da Udine.

After visiting the Sistine Chapel, we can spend a little time looking at the **Collection of Modern Religious Art**.

Consisting of famous paintings and sculptures only recently assembled here by Paul VI (in 1973), it is displayed in a total of 55 rooms, and includes works by Modigliani, Matisse, Le Corbusier, Chagall, Gauguin and others.

The Borgia Apartment - Hall of the mysteries of Faith (Pinturicchio)

The Vatican Library

Founded by Pope Sixtus IV in 1475, the Vatican collection was marked by a rapid increase in the number of books it contained. Between 1587 and 1589 Sixtus V commissioned the architect **Domenico Fontana** to build a large hall, the **Sistine Hall**, to house it. It consists of two aisles divided by seven pillars and decorated with frescoes depicting scenes from the pontificate of Sixtus V. The apostolic collection contains a valuable collection of illuminated manuscripts, as well as codices and printed books.

Of the 13 rooms that compose the Vatican Library, we may mention Room I or **Museo Profano**, which houses Etruscan and Roman artefacts; Room X, known as the **Sala delle Nozze Aldobrandini**, in which ancient frescoes are displayed including that of the « Aldobrandine Nuptials » after which the room is named; and Room XII or **Chapel of Pius V**, decorated by Jacopo Zucchi.

The Vatican Library

Castel Gandolfo

Situated not far from Rome, this characteristic little hill-town and resort is especially famous because it is the summer residence of the Pope. The surrounding landscape is very picturesque, thanks to the presence of the charming Lake Albano — the ancient Lacus Albanus — over which Castel Gandolfo stands. At the centre of the town is the Piazza della Libertà, adorned by a fountain designed by Bernini. At the end of the piazza is the Papal Palace (17th century).

Designed by the architect Maderno, it was erected under the pontificate of Urban VIII on the site of the ancient Castle of the Savelli and later transformed. The façade is adorned with an elegant balcony (the Loggia from which the Pope gives his blessing) surmounted by a clock, and the coat of arms of Alexander VII. The interior of the palace, much changed by Pius IX, is richly decorated with stuccoes and frescoes. The Vatican Observatory annexed to it is considered one of the most important astronomical observatories in Europe. A few steps from the building we can ascend to a panoramic terrace, from where we can enjoy a wonderful view of the lake below.

One side of the piazza is delimited by the church of San Tommaso di Villanova, by Bernini, who also designed the fine dome by which it is surmounted. It contains some fine altarpieces by Maratta («Assumption»); Pietro da Cortona («St. Thomas of Villanova»); and Antonio Raggi, who was also responsible for the stuccoes that decorate the dome.

Liberty Square and Papal Palace

Pontifical Gardens and Palace

Tivoli - The Villa d'Este

Tivoli lies some 30 km from Rome: it is a town of great antiquity, full of interesting reminders of its past, first and foremost the **Villa d'Este**. The villa, famous especially for its garden and the many fountains with which it is embellished, was built by Pirro Ligorio in 1550. The garden consists of two distinct parts joined by three large fishponds and by the Fountain of Neptune. The part of the garden on the slopes of the hill on which the villa lies is divided by a series of paths on which a number of charming fountains are laid out, such as the Fountain of the Dragon (at the centre of the first avenue), flanked by the Fountains of Proserpine and the Organ: the Fountain of Tivoli, the so-called Hundred Fountains and the Fontana del Bicchierone, to which Bernini also contributed. In the lower part of the gardens are mock-grottoes with themes of fantasy. In the centre of Tivoli it is worth visiting the Cathedral, an interesting baroque building begun in the 17th century but completed only much later; it is flanked by a fine Romanesque bell-tower.

Villa d'Este - The Ovato's Fountain

Villa d'Este - The Organ's Fountain ➤

Villa d'Este - Hundred Fountaines alley

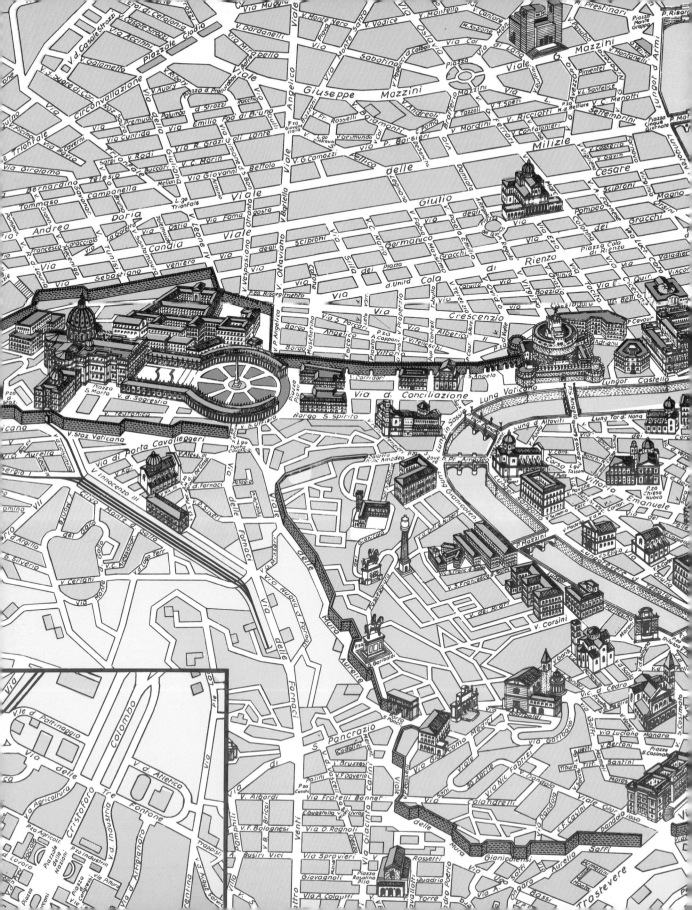

INDEX

PHOTOGRAPHS:

© Archivio Plurigraf
Foto aeree concess. S.M.A. 1257 del 21-12-92.
Foto Le Clic, pag. 46a.
C. Gerolimetto, pag. 48.
Arte e Immagini, pag. 108-109-110-111-112.

© Copyright by Casa Editrice Plurigraf
S.S. Flaminia, km 90 - 05035 Narni - Terni - Italia
Tel. 0744 / 715946 - Fax 0744 / 722540 - (Italy country code: +39)
All rights reserved. No Part of this publication may be reproduced.
Printed: 1996 - Plurigraf S.p.A. - Narni

L. 12.000
I.V.A. INCLUSA